The Real Smith Wigglesworth

The Man, The Myth, The Message

Desmond Cartwright

Sovereign World

Sovereign World Ltd
PO Box 777
Tonbridge
Kent
TN11 0ZS
England

Scripture quotations:
NIV – HOLY BIBLE, NEW INTERNATIONAL VERSION. Copyright ©
1973, 1978, 1984 by International Bible Society. Used by permission.
AV – Authorised Version. Crown copyright.

ISBN 1 85240 280 6

The publishers aim to produce books which will help to extend and
build up the Kingdom of God. We do not necessarily agree with every
view expressed by the author, or with every interpretation of Scripture
expressed. We expect each reader to make his/her judgement in the
light of their own understanding of God's Word and in an attitude of
Christian love and fellowship.

Typeset by CRB Associates, Reepham, Norfolk.
Printed in England by Clays Ltd, St Ives plc.

Contents

Introduction

In the unfolding story of the moving of God's Holy Spirit through the Pentecostal and Charismatic outpourings of the past 100 years, Smith Wigglesworth stands as a colossus. The life and ministry of this Yorkshire plumber have inspired countless thousands. With his insistence on simple and absolute faith, Smith Wigglesworth has been heralded as one of the fathers of the Pentecostal and Charismatic movements, The Word of Faith Movement and of other streams and denominations which have longed for the restoration of a church of supernatural and miraculous power.

In recent years there has been something of a Wigglesworth publishing industry. It seems that there is a tremendous appetite throughout the body of Christ for information and testimony concerning the ministry of Smith Wigglesworth. Stories abound of amazing healings, even more remarkable creative miracles and bold unorthodox methods.

Written by my father, Desmond, official historian of the Elim Pentecostal Churches and founding archivist of the Donald Gee Centre for Pentecostal and Charismatic Research at Mattersey College, this volume seeks to present a fresh picture of Smith Wigglesworth and to tease out some of the challenges that we face in understanding and assessing the impact of this extraordinary man of faith. With access to the fullest collection of source materials, including previously unpublished letters, reports of meetings, and sermons, *The Real Smith Wigglesworth* offers a major contribution to the Wigglesworth literature and helps to broaden our understanding of the man and his ministry.

At times Smith Wigglesworth's ministry seems of almost mythical proportions. Certainly there have been great difficulties experienced by historians and writers in establishing a credible and factual account both of the details of Wigglesworth's biography and of the reports and claims of the extraordinary testimonies which followed him wherever he went. There is a considerable amount of anecdotal information passed around particularly in sermon illustrations. Though fascinating, many of these anecdotes are undocumented and therefore difficult to verify. This volume seeks to add a wealth of previously unavailable accounts and, wherever possible, to illustrate something of the lifestyle, character and methods of ministry of Smith Wigglesworth.

There are a number of myths to be shattered. Firstly, as you go through this account you will see that contrary to what may have been suggested, Wigglesworth clearly could read and write. It would be true to say that he was uninterested in newspapers, magazines, or reading anything other than the Bible. He treasured and preserved an inner life with God that would allow no interruptions from what he saw as mere worldly things. Lester Sumrall tells the story of arriving at his home to visit with a newspaper under his arm and Wigglesworth brusquely saying, 'you can come in but the newspaper stays outside.' This was one of many indications that Smith was a man who sought nothing more than the presence of the Lord. Certainly he was an awesome figure and many were in a sense a little afraid of him. Yet, just a moment or two in his presence would convince people of his sincere love of the Lord and his compassion and tenderness for people. Although he was never a sophisticated speaker or writer, he certainly had a way of getting his point across. Some of the letters, which are included in this volume, are priceless in their passion and simplicity and throw much light on how Wigglesworth viewed the ministry that God had given him.

The second myth that this volume seeks to explode is that we can look to Wigglesworth for clear and accurate prophecies of our times. There has been much made of his prophesying an 'end time move of God' and, more specifically many have referred to a prophecy given by him to David du Plessis. I think responsibly in *The Real Smith Wigglesworth*, we are encouraged not so much to look for the exact letter of an undocumented prophetic utterance given by Wigglesworth years ago, but rather to understand his general belief in an end time move of God which he demonstrably believed would usher in the second coming of the Lord Jesus Christ.

More than anything else, I believe that Wigglesworth emerges from these pages as characteristically a vessel of honour in the hands of the Master. Our prayer as you read this book is that you will not simply be inspired by the life of a great man, but drawn closer to the Lord Jesus Himself. For Wigglesworth to truly be a pioneer, as many have claimed him to be, we must look to be a generation who will follow him into the fullness of all that God promises to do through His church. We must become a people of faith who will take the mantle or baton handed us by those who have gone before and who will run our race with great faith for a great harvest.

Chris Cartwright
City Temple, Cardiff.

Preface

'Why another book about Wigglesworth?' someone may ask. Well, in a few words I will give my reasons for writing.

Like many others, I had heard a great deal about Smith Wigglesworth. I was first introduced to him very shortly after my conversion in 1949, two years after his death. His first biography, published in 1949, was written by Stanley Frodsham, an English-born writer who was editor of the American Assemblies of God magazine, *Pentecostal Evangel*, from 1920 to 1949. Though he met Wigglesworth on his first visit to the USA in 1914 and in several places in Britain before that time, he acknowledged that the major part of the book was owed to Wigglesworth's son-in-law, James Salter, and his wife Alice.

Since this first biography there have also been several others. Some of these, though somewhat brief, were written by men who had met Wigglesworth. In addition to these accounts, however, there is now material available which, to my knowledge, has never been previously used (except in a journal article that I wrote and which one writer has since quoted). This includes the considerable number of reprints of his sermons. One collection alone runs to more than 800 pages and contains some 158 sermons delivered between 1914 and the 1940s.[1] But even this does not contain all of his recorded sermons; there are at least sixteen more that cover the period between 1916 and 1937. More importantly, there are detailed reports of his meetings in magazines and newspapers, both religious and secular, the vast majority of which are not to be found in any of the previous books. Added to this there is a considerable collection of letters in Wigglesworth's own handwriting and others are still being discovered.

I have written for the general reader rather than for the scholar (though I can give full references to substantiate all that I have related). I have made use of contemporary material wherever this has been available and, as far as possible, have quoted directly from this. Some of the stories about Smith Wigglesworth are in my opinion exaggerated and a small number strain credulity beyond legitimate limits. The true and genuine stories about Wigglesworth, authenticated in some cases by hundreds of witnesses, do not need further support from doubtful cases.

What we discover in our look at the life and ministry of Smith Wigglesworth is a simple, humble man who wanted the best that God had to offer. He was a man who was prepared to open his heart to seek out God's best in the company of godly men and women wherever they were to be found. Though he was frequently linked with small, despised and frequently misunderstood groups he was never in any sense a narrow sectarian. His lifelong pilgrimage would bring him into contact with Christians of many different persuasions: Methodist, Anglican, Brethren, Salvation Army, Holiness and Pentecostal.

In all of the letters and any other contemporary material relating to Smith Wigglesworth that made their way to 70 Victor Road, Bradford – his home for some forty years –

he would never be addressed as 'Smith' but always as Mr Wigglesworth. In a few cases we have observed that some writers have been a little confused and have added a hyphen referring to him as Smith-Wigglesworth. Such names are normally associated with the English aristocracy, a group to which Wigglesworth never belonged and to which he never aspired. He was born into an ordinary working-class family. He was in some ways to remain a working man all his life. He was for a time the leader of a small mission in Bradford, Yorkshire, and held credentials with the American Assemblies of God during their infancy but he was never officially attached to any denomination but moved freely among many groups. He was in fact a layman and remained so to the end of his days. Wigglesworth was happy to describe himself as Pentecostal.

Wigglesworth was born a few years before the introduction of compulsory schooling which was first introduced in England in 1870. Such evidence that we have, based upon more than thirty original handwritten letters penned over a period of more than twenty years, reveal to us that Wigglesworth was quite capable of writing. There is very little in his letters by way of punctuation; the spelling is erratic but the intention is always clear. Those to whom he wrote were often men of superior education, lawyers, clergymen and others.

Wigglesworth addressed large gatherings of students and coped with ease with questions that were fired at him. Some of the stories that have been told about his lack of learning ought to be confined to the realm of fiction. One writer tells of a student who, on meeting him, said, 'Mr Wigglesworth, when you wrote to me you spelt "Holy Ghost" six different ways.' Wigglesworth apparently retorted, 'Did you understand what I was saying?' to which the student replied, 'Yes.' 'Then,' Wigglesworth replied, 'that is all that matters.' It's a good story, though I'm rather disposed to question its accuracy. Not only is it irreverent but it is quite difficult, if not impossible, to spell Holy Ghost in such a variety of different ways!

He regularly convened large meetings with ease for many years and mixed easily in the company of those with whom, in the natural world of his time, he would have only viewed at a respectful distance. Once, when speaking at a meeting he used a very convoluted sentence. Someone in the audience, a little confused, called out, 'Brother, can you repeat that?' 'No,' said Wigglesworth, 'I'll give you something better.'

He touched hundreds during his lifetime, even thousands. Since his death in 1947 his sermons and the stories about him have touched and inspired countless more. He was a bold and fearless witness for his Lord and would use every opportunity to witness no matter what company he was in. As an evangelist he faced large crowds and frequently challenged men and women to make a public confession of Christ. As he travelled in many parts of the world, in Britain, the USA, South Africa, New Zealand or Australia, he would buttonhole people with a word of witness. In the first class railway carriage he would share a word with a businessman and confront him with the claims of Christ or share a prayer. A number of years ago when I was taking lessons from a former senior advanced driving instructor the man gave me a photograph of Smith Wigglesworth. He never told me where he acquired the picture but I suspect that he, or one of his family, had been healed through Wigglesworth's ministry.

Wigglesworth was greatly used in healing and there were constant demands for his services even when he was at a very advanced age. He never set up any corporation or organisation. He had no mailing lists and sent out no 'prayer letters' to his supporters. He was content to leave the work in the Master's hand. In contrast to many others who worked in the same field, he never kept lists of names or published the photographs of those who were healed as a result of his ministrations. His memorial is in the inspiration of his life and its insistence on faith.

I am grateful to those other writers who have trodden this path before me. One of the writers, the late George Stormont, baptised me within a few months of my conversion. Other writers, like my friends Jack Hywel-Davies and Robert Liardon, who between them represent the older and younger elements of the interest in Wigglesworth, have both plied me with questions over the years. I am grateful to them for, in some cases, their questions stimulated me to make further inquiries which eventually led to the writing of this book.

Two sources were especially helpful. I spent many hours with members of the Wigglesworth family, in particular with his grandson Leslie and his wife, Ruth, who was one of E.C.W. Boulton's daughters. They shared many stories with me, not only about their grandfather but many of his friends and associates. The best source by far, however, has been the Donald Gee Centre for Pentecostal and Charismatic Research. It has been my privilege to serve as archivist there for some ten years. I am especially grateful to the Principal of Mattersey Hall, Dr David Petts, firstly for having the foresight to provide accommodation for what has proved such a valuable collection, and secondly for giving his encouragement to the ongoing work of the Centre. Although this collection of books, magazines, letters and much other material associated with the history of Pentecostalism is housed in the Assemblies of God College it is managed by a group of independent trustees who represent that wider spectrum which British Pentecostalism now embraces. There are letters to and from Smith Wigglesworth and the most complete run of Alexander Boddy's paper *Confidence*, produced from 1908 to 1926, as well as a full set of *Redemption Tidings* from 1924.

If my readers enjoy reading about Smith Wigglesworth as much as I have enjoyed researching and writing this book my effort will have been worthwhile. He served God in his generation. After he died a new generation arose to meet the challenge of a rapidly changing world. Pentecostalism grew and expanded in ways that would have probably astounded the old warrior. There have been some aspects about which he would have made more than a few blunt comments. Whether or not he uttered the words now being attributed to him is still an open question. There can be no doubt, however, that he believed in and prayed for a global expansion of the work of God. As much as he was used in healing, his chief concern was for the salvation of sinners and the building up of God's people. He was indeed the Apostle of Faith.

Desmond Cartwright

Note

1. Roberts Liardon, *Smith Wigglesworth: The Complete Collection of His Life and Teaching* (Tulsa, Oklahoma, USA: Albury Publishing, 1996).

Chapter 1

Beginnings

The story we have to tell began in the momentous year 1859. It was the year that saw the publication of Charles Darwin's *Origin of the Species*. In the same year, when Charles Dickens wrote *A Tale of Two Cities*, he penned one of the most famous opening lines in literature. Describing the French Revolution of 1789, he wrote, 'It was the best of times, it was the worst of times.'

It was also the year that ushered in what became known as the Second Evangelical Awakening in Britain. The Christian newspaper, *The Revival*, later renamed *The Christian*, was launched in this same year to record the details of these events. It was a momentous year.

Against this backcloth, on Friday 10 June 1859,[1] in the small village of Menston, ten miles from Bradford in Yorkshire, a second son was born to Martha and John Wigglesworth. The boy was named Smith. We do not know why he was given that name, but it was not unusual in Yorkshire for sons to be given what was usually a surname as a Christian name.

Menston was a small rural community. At the time of the National Census in 1861 the population was recorded as only 318. Ten years later it had risen to 455, and as the nineteenth century proceeded, it continued to expand slowly. In 1865 the railway came to Warfedale, attracting woolmen and cloth merchants from Leeds and Bradford into the district. The Anglicans had no church in Menston but met in a cottage until they were able to establish their own church building in 1871. By 1881 the propulation had risen to 662 and ten years later to 1,742.

The family

The Wigglesworth family lived in obscurity as their ancestors had done for generations before. It might have remained so but for the faith of grandmother Bella. It is from this grand old lady, born in 1778, that we can trace a line back to the time of John Wesley (1703–91) and the beginnings of Methodism which left such a mark in Yorkshire as it also did on many other places in the eighteenth century.

John Wesley visited Bradford on at least twenty occasions between 1741 and 1790. The history of Methodism in Menston dates back to 1744 when meetings were conducted in private homes. In 1826, when the population of the village was less than 300, land was given for the erection of a Methodist chapel, and this building still stands alongside the larger building that was erected in 1886. It became affectionately known as 't'owd chapel' and was noted for its revival atmosphere.

When John Wesley visited Bradford in August 1778, the year that Smith's grandmother was born, he noted in his *Journal* that the congregation had grown to such an extent that he had the largest crowd since leaving London. John Wesley and his associates had been very active in Yorkshire and had seen great success in the county. His final visit was made in the summer of 1790 when he was eighty-seven

years of age. It is highly likely that young Bella was amongst
the crowd who heard the ancient patriarch that day.
Thus we have a link between John Wesley and Smith
Wigglesworth. Not that there was any physical resemblance
between them. Wesley was diminutive in size and frail
looking although obviously tough and wiry. Wigglesworth, though he was of average height, was a physically
strong man with large hands and possessing a powerful
voice.

At the time of the 1861 Census, Bella Wigglesworth was
an 83-year-old widow living at 21 Burley Lane with her son,
Richard, and three grandchildren. She was an active
member of the nearby Wesleyan chapel in Stocks Hill. The
old lady took a lively interest in all her family but she
seemed to have taken a special interest in Smith. When he
was a child of eight years of age he accompanied her to one
of those very lively old Methodist meetings. It was in this
meeting that he made his first act of commitment to Christ.

Having been christened in the Church of England when
he was six months old, in September 1872 Smith was
confirmed at the usual age of thirteen. Many years later he
would speak of having first experienced the power of the
Holy Spirit, which he then knew in much fuller measure,
when the bishop laid hands on him. That same year the
family moved to nearby Bradford which, along with Leeds,
was experiencing a rapid population explosion. Bradford
was to become synonymous with the name of Smith
Wigglesworth for some forty years.

Bradford

At first Wigglesworth renewed his association with the
Methodists but three years later, when the Salvation Army

entered Bradford, he began to attend their meetings. William Booth had originally belonged to a branch of the Methodist Church and Smith found their bold and aggressive form of evangelism very attractive. In a short time he was to discover that one of the Salvation Army lasses was irresistible, and in 1882 he married Mary Jane Featherstone (nicknamed Polly). The Salvation Army hall in Shipley, on the outskirts of Bradford, still carries a foundation stone dated 5 November 1892 bearing the name Mr Wigglesworth. It is the only memorial to his name in the area.

With the move to Bradford, Smith found employment in a textile mill where he was befriended by a member of the Brethren. This unnamed brother taught him plumbing but, more importantly, introduced him to the importance of believers' baptism. As a result he was baptised by immersion. He also made acquaintance with a group of people in the nearby town of Leeds who believed in and practised what they called divine healing. The exact date and some of the details here are still a little vague but it is very clear that this new contact was to steer Wigglesworth's ministry in a direction that would make his name famous even many years after his death.

Divine healing

In the first place Wigglesworth himself experienced a touch from God in his body. He does not tell us what the condition was from which he suffering, but by his own account it would appear to have been serious and particularly debilitating. In a newspaper report of a meeting in Old Colwyn in September 1925, we read that he told the congregation that 'Thirty-five years ago I was a weakling, helpless, and dying, when God in a single moment healed me. I am now sixty-six and as fresh as any of you and as ready for work as I ever was.'[2] This would make the date some time in 1890.

The group Wigglesworth contacted at this time was most probably led by Mrs Elizabeth Baxter[3] and her husband Richard Paget Baxter,[4] the founders and proprietors of the *Christian Herald*. Mr Baxter (1834–1910) took a great deal of interest in prophetic subjects and wrote extensively. He was known as 'Prophet Baxter' and had founded the Prophetic Society in 1872. He also launched the magazine *Prophetic News* and *Israel's Messenger*. He was a great philanthropist and gave support to many worthy causes. His biographer has said that he probably gave away some £70,000 to worthy causes during his lifetime. That is a large amount even today, but in the period before the First World War it was a huge sum. One of these causes was the Gospel Union and Blue Ribbon Army founded by R.I. Booth and William Noble. In the period between January 1882 and 31 May 1885 Mr Baxter seems to have been the chief financial backer of the work which strongly advocated temperance, spending almost £20,000 in sustaining it.

There is yet another strand that helps us to build up a picture of the Christian world in which Smith and Polly Wigglesworth engaged much of their spare time. John Alexander Dowie (1847–1907) had a remarkable ministry of healing which had begun during an epidemic in Australia in 1876. He was the founder of Zion City near Chicago, which was established as a sort of Utopia with great emphasis placed on healing. He had contact with Mrs Baxter and she had published a letter from him in her paper, *The Healer*, in 1885, in which he said that he hoped to be present at a conference that was to be held at the Agricultural Hall, Islington in London, on the subject of divine healing, in that year. In the event Dowie did not come on that occasion but in 1900 he held several meetings in London at Clapham, Hornsey and Islington. The meetings he held were highly publicised and even the prestigious *Financial Times* had something to say on the matter. Our interest is in the fact that amongst those who were baptised by trine immersion by Dowie at that time was 'Mrs M.J. Wigglesworth of Bradford'.

Following the Zion City meetings in London a work was established in London led by Harry Eugene Cantel, with his wife, Margaret, who was the daughter of one of the elders at Zion City. After their marriage in 1907 they returned to London where they set up one of the earliest Pentecostal Assemblies in the city, publishing the newspaper *The Overcoming Life* from February 1909. The newspaper ran from that time until Harry Cantel's premature death from peritonitis in August 1910.

As far as we know there was no Zion work in Bradford but the Wigglesworths were in regular contact with a small Zion meeting in nearby Leeds. A few years later, following meetings conducted by Elim evangelist George Jeffreys, first in 1913 and subsequently in 1920 and 1927, this would become the Bridge Street Elim Church.

Polly and Smith also found considerable help from the work of Reader Harris QC, leader of the Pentecostal League of Prayer. This was a small but intense holiness group, initially transdenominational, with a network of some 150 groups and a membership of about 17,000. Their main centre was at Speake Hall, Battersea, London, which Harris purchased in 1887 and named a 'Pentecostal Mission', but they had other centres throughout the country. Among the meeting places listed in their paper, *Tongues of Fire*, was Bowland Street Mission, Manningham, Bradford where the leaders were Mr and Mrs Smith Wigglesworth. Another of the meetings listed was one of several in Sunderland where the leader was the vicar of All Saints Monkwearmouth, Rev. Alexander Boddy (1854–1930). He and Wigglesworth would share a great deal more within a few years.

Notes

1. There is some slight confusion about the date of Smith Wigglesworth's birth. Earlier biographers differ by two days. James Salter, his son-in-law, said in reporting his death that he would have been eighty-eight if he had lived until 8 June. Others have given 10 June as the date. Such confusion is not unusual, particularly where birth certificates are not carefully kept. It is highly probable that he had observed the one date and it was only later, probably when he needed to obtain a passport, that he found out the correct date. I have been able to verify that the correct date was 10 June. This was confirmed by his granddaughter, Mrs Hobbs whose daughter was born on 10 June 1947, which was Smith Wigglesworth's 87th birthday.

2. *Redemption Tidings* 1, 9 September 1925, p. 11. See also *North Wales Weekly News*, 10 September 1925.

3. Nathaniel Wiseman, *Elizabeth Baxter (Wife of Michael Paget Baxter) Saint, Evangelist, Teacher and Expositor* (second edition, 1928).

4. Nathaniel Wiseman, *Michael Paget Baxter: Clergyman-Evangelist, Editor and Philanthropist* (Chas. J. Thyne and Jarvis, 1923). Michael was the son of Robert Baxter b. 1802, the Doncaster lawyer who was for a few years associated with Edward Irving's London congregation. The family were descended from a brother of the more famous Richard Baxter, author of *The Reformed Pastor*.

All Saints' Vicarage and Church, Fulwell Road, Monkwearmouth, Sunderland

Rev. Alexander Boddy with his wife and two daughters

Chapter 2

Revival

In the winter of 1904–5 a great religious revival had broken out in Wales under the ministry of Evan Roberts (1878–1951) and others. As a result some one hundred thousand conversions were recorded.

There was a widespread coverage of these meetings in both the secular and Christian press at the time, drawing visitors to Wales from many parts. One such visitor in the Spring of 1906 was a doctor, specialising in psychiatry, who had been commissioned by the French Home Office to report on the revival and investigate the effects of 'religious excitement' on those suffering from nervous instability. His report on behalf of the French Public Health Department, which extended to almost two hundred pages, gave a sympathetic and fair-minded account of what he witnessed, though the revival had passed its zenith by the time he arrived.

The Vicar

Another visitor to Wales was Vicar Boddy from Sunderland. In spite of the fact that he had served in an industrial parish for some twenty years, Boddy was widely travelled, having visited the USA and Canada as well as having spent time in Egypt, North Africa and Russia. He had written several books describing his travels and adventures which included a journey to one of the holy sites of Islam, Kairwan, where he had gone in disguise, having taken the precaution of arming himself with a revolver.

On this occasion, the reason for his visit was more than mere curiosity. Boddy records that, during his travels, a stranger he had met on a train on one occasion had said to him, 'Brother, put first things first.' The words made a deep impact on him. Son of a minister, he had been a lawyer before training for the ministry at Durham under Bishop Lightfoot and, by his own admission, had lived his spiritual life at a very low level for a number of years. He had begun to seek ways to bring it onto a higher plane and visits to the Keswick Convention had proved of some assistance, but it was not until September 1892, while conducting the service for St Matthew's Day, that he received an assurance and the inward witness of the Holy Spirit of full salvation. From that time the direction of his future travels would be given a spiritual priority.

Now, in December 1904 Alexander Boddy travelled by train from Sunderland to Tonypandy in the Rhondda where he met Evan Roberts. What he saw and heard made a great impression on him. He was greatly helped by personal contact with Evan Roberts who, after a meeting in Tonypandy, told him, 'Tell them to believe the promise, believe the Book. They must fight heaven down. Bring it down now and here. Fight it down.'

On his return he began special meetings in his own church and a number were converted. Boddy was also active in promoting teaching on holiness and was the local secretary for the interdenominational group in Sunderland known as the Pentecostal League of Prayer founded by Reader Harris QC with which Smith Wigglesworth was also connected (see Chapter 1). The League's combined membership at one time was some 17,000, and they sold more copies of their newspaper *Tongues of Fire* in Sunderland than in any other town. Though Harris used the title 'Pentecostal' for his meetings, as others also did, these meetings were not Pentecostal in the sense in which this phrase was to be used later.

A new movement

The American writer and missionary statesman, Arthur T. Pierson (1837–1911), writing in *Forward Movements in the Last Half-Century* in 1900, had a chapter entitled 'The Pentecostal Movement', which told the story of a short-lived revival in Uganda under the ministry of George Lawrence Pilkington, a Church Missionary Society missionary martyred in 1897. Dublin-born Pilkington, a promising classical scholar who was converted in 1885 and went to Uganda in 1890, taught the necessity of the experience of the baptism of the Holy Spirit. This movement was not 'Pentecostal', however, in the same sense as the small beginnings of a work of God soon to emerge in middle America.

At a theological college in Topeka, Kansas, students, under the guidance of Charles Parham, were studying the subject of the baptism of the Holy Spirit at their watch-night services. The phrase 'the baptism of the Holy Spirit' was used originally by John the Baptist when he explained to his disciples that someone else, more worthy than he, would come who would baptise them with the Holy Spirit and with fire. This promise was repeated to the disciples by Jesus when He appeared to them after the resurrection. Ten days later, in the city of Jerusalem, the promised Spirit descended upon the waiting company of some one hundred and twenty people. The external evidence of the presence of the Spirit was that the men and women present spoke in tongues.[1] The name for this is glossolalia, a technical term derived from a combination of two Greek words meaning to speak in or by tongues. The question that Charles Parham raised with his students was this, 'What is the biblical evidence that a person has been baptised in the Holy Spirit?' The question was simple. The answers had been elusive. They would become controversial. One answer would become first decisive and then divisive. It would give birth to what would become known as the Pentecostal/Charismatic Movement. Starting with one person on 1 January 1901, the first day of the century, by the end of the century a phenomenal 500 million believers would have shared this experience, representing an estimated 29 per cent of Christendom.

Reports of the revival in Wales had been taken back to the United States by Christian workers who had been to see what was happening for themselves. There was also widespread coverage in the Christian press. Among the visitors was Joseph Smale, a former student of Spurgeon's College, who was a pastor of the First Baptist Church in Los Angeles. He went to see the Welsh revival for himself and on his return called for special prayer that such a revival might take place in their town.

In April 1906, through the ministry of William Joseph Seymour, a former student of Charles Parham, a special outpouring of the Holy Spirit began in Los Angeles. One of the first to experience speaking in tongues at that time was

Jennie Evans Moore, who was a member of Joseph Smale's church. Two years later she married Seymour and they set up their home in a former stable that was to become known as the Azusa Street Mission. Over the next three years many Christian workers went to this meeting place seeking a deeper experience through the Holy Spirit.

In September 1906 a new large format newspaper entitled *Apostolic Faith* was issued from Azusa Street. This newspaper would have an enormous influence over the next two years. Eventually, more than 50,000 copies would be printed and its message carried to the ends of the earth. On the other side of the country in New York, an English-born Methodist minister, Thomas B. Barratt, was on a visit to the States seeking to raise funds for his city mission in Oslo. The trip had not been a great success and Barratt faced a crisis. Staying at the Christian Alliance home of A.B. Simpson in New York he happened to read the *Apostolic Faith* newspaper. As a result he began to seek God more earnestly which led him to write to the leaders of the Azusa Street Mission. On Sunday 7 October, in his room in the Alliance house, he experienced a special anointing of the Spirit. Further communications with Los Angeles led him to go deeper and on 14 November, at a mission on Fourteenth Street, he spoke in tongues for the first time. Describing this experience, Barratt, a musician who had trained under Edvard Greig, told how he spoke in what he regarded as seven or eight different languages. He also gave a vivid description of singing in the Spirit:

'The most beautiful of all was the singing – when the inspiration reached a climax, I burst out in a wonderful baritone solo. I never heard the tune before, and did not understand the words, but it was a most beautiful language, so smooth and easy to pronounce. Those who were present and heard the whole thing, said that my voice was quite changed. I never forgot how beautiful and pure the singing sounded. It seemed to me the rhythm in the verses and chorus, was as perfect as it is possible to be.'

Early in December, Barratt returned to Norway where the news of his new experience had preceded him and he was greeted by a mixture of considerable excitement and deep scepticism. He would later become the father of European Pentecostalism with a ministry that would have far-reaching implications. It was his contact and influence that brought the Swedish Baptist pastor, Lewi Pethrus (1884–1974) into the Pentecostal Movement. More importantly, for our present interest, was his influence on the English clergyman, Alexander Boddy.

Reports of what was happening in Norway appeared in the missionary paper, the *South African Pioneer*. As a result, Alexander Boddy decided to visit Oslo to see things for himself. What he saw there left a deeper impression on him than even that which he had observed during his visit to the Rhondda Valley and his meeting with Evan Roberts at the height of the Welsh Revival. Now Boddy urged Barratt to visit his Sunderland parish at the earliest opportunity.

Barratt arrived in Sunderland on the last day of August 1907 and stayed for a period of some seven weeks. During this time a number of Christian workers were baptised in the Spirit and spoke in tongues. Among them was Alexander Boddy's wife Mary, who had missed the first two Sundays of Barratt's visit due to being away in the south of England. She spoke in tongues for the first time on

11 September. The couple's two daughters, Mary (14) and
Jane (15) also shared in the experience on 21 September.
During Barratt's visit some seventeen people spoke in
tongues. After about a month the newspapers picked up
the story and from then on the vicarage was besieged with
curious reporters and eager seekers. Boddy had to wait until
2 December before receiving the gift for himself. He wrote
to Mrs Jessie Penn-Lewis, a lady associated with Evan
Roberts and who, together with her husband, provided
Roberts with a home in Leicester after he suffered a break-
down. Boddy explained in simple terms:

> 'Will you rejoice with me (1 Cor. 12:26) because the
> Lord in His infinite compassion has now given me
> the seal of the Tongues (Acts 10:46; 11:15; 15:9; Rev.
> 7:3; 2 Cor. 1:21)?
>
> Last night (Monday Decr. 2nd) in our Meeting in the
> Vestry (about 100 present) as soon as He had spoken
> clearly through me and filled us with joy He graciously
> used me to Bro. Tetchner (S.A.) who has been with me
> "seeking" all the time – and we were soon rejoicing
> together as the Lord gave him the sign also. I am the
> 50th here to receive the Sign of the Tongues (pente-
> cost means "Fiftieth"). Seven have been thus blessed
> this week-end. Hallelujah for ever to the Lamb that
> was slain who redeemed us by His blood.
>
> A.A.B.'   *(reproduced exactly as written)*

These events in Sunderland really gave birth to the
Pentecostal Movement in Britain. From 1907 to the outbreak of the First World War, Alexander Boddy was to play
a leading part in that growth and development. It is,

however, to another visitor to these meetings that we turn in our next chapter.

Note

1.   See Mark 1:8; Acts 1:4–5; 2:1–4.

Chapter 3

Changed Lives

At the turn of the century Smith Wigglesworth was well established in Bradford where he had a good reputation as an honest and hard-working tradesman. He was also active in Christian work, and he and his wife had been engaged in evangelistic mission for a number of years.

On Saturday 13 February 1904 an event took place in Bowland Street Mission which had important repercussions. James Berry (1862–1913) had been Public Executioner from 1884 to 1892 and had been responsible for the hanging of 134 men and women. After his resignation he was given to bouts of depression and had taken to drink. One day, in a fit of black despair, he was sitting on the platform of the Midland Station in Bradford contemplating taking his life, when he was approached by a young man, a recent convert from Bowland Street. The young man engaged him in conversation and Berry in desperation poured out his heart in a flood of tears. The young man asked him to come to the mission later in the afternoon where he would introduce him to friends who would give him further help. Returning home, Berry told his wife what had taken place and, though she was not herself religious, she prayed that he would be delivered from the curse of drink. When he arrived at the mission there were shouts of victory and for the next hour or more everyone joined in praying and praising as Berry fully surrendered his life to God. The former executioner rose to his feet filled with joy and praise. He asked some of the people from the mission to accompany him to his home in Bilton Place where, much to his wife's astonishment, he explained what had happened to him. Mrs Berry was herself converted and gave herself to Christ. There was, however, an unusual interruption to the proceedings. Mrs Berry, in an attempt to keep her husband indoors and to prevent him spending too much time and money at the public house, had ordered a barrel of beer to be delivered to the house. It arrived during their meeting. Berry immediately sent the deliveryman packing. It was an experience as dramatic as the conversion of the jailer at Philippi in Acts 16.

Berry, who had been brought up as a Wesleyan Methodist, was now anxious to share the story of his new experience. He was soon taken on as a missioner by the Primitive Methodists and he began with ten days in Edinburgh. He stayed in Scotland for several months where his services were in great demand. Later, this time accompanied by his wife, he travelled all over England and more than 500 conversions were recorded. The former executioner became a changed man in every way. The rest of his life was devoted to advocating temperance, evangelism and arguing against capital punishment. Strangely his story is to be found recorded on a tract that was deposited in the Chamber of Horrors at Madame Tussaud's. Thus Wigglesworth is found in some strange places.

Wigglesworth's own story

When the news of what had been taking place in Sunderland during the visit of the Methodist minister from Norway, T.B. Barratt, became public in October 1907, Smith Wigglesworth decided to go to Sunderland to see what was happening. He arrived there on the last weekend in October and, wishing to fill his time, attended meetings in the local Salvation Army hall as well as the Anglican church. In his written testimony, first published as a separate tract in November 1907 and printed by Alexander Boddy in his newspaper *Confidence* in November 1908 he gives us some of the details of the story:

'For three months I have been exercised about the full Pentecost. I had a clear witness of the Baptism of the Holy Spirit 14 years ago last July [1894], and this brought a marvellous manifestation of God in special gifts to the sick ones, and a constant living and seeking to bring others to Jesus. But from time to time when reading the Acts of the Apostles I always saw that the signs were not following as I am led to believe ought to be after real Pentecost, according to Mark 16. The desire more and more increased in my very inner soul, giving me a holy breathing cry after this clear manifestation. I had visited meetings at London, and Sunderland, and other places, but always knew that they were not seeking Pentecosts. There seemed a great deal of letter, but very little of the spirit that would give the hungry and needy the Baptism of Fire such as would burn up distinctions and officiousness and appearance of Pride and evidence of social standing.

Today I am actually living in the Acts of the Apostles' time, I am speaking with new tongues, the Holy Fire of God's Presence fills me till my pen moves to the glory of God, and my whole being is filled with the Presence of the Holy Ghost. Almost I am led to believe that 20 years is not too long to wait for the Holy Anointing of God the Holy Ghost.'

He then gives us the details of how this took place:

'On Friday, 25th, we had a special meeting at the Mission Room, Bowland Street, Bradford, and after waiting about two hours the Presence of God came in a wonderful way and gave me a move as at the beginning. I perfectly well understood the glow and Holy Presence. This was felt by others also. On Saturday, I and a friend went on to Sunderland to wait for Pentecost at All Saints', at Mr. Boddy's church. We had heard much about this blessed work and were encouraged, but after arriving at Sunderland found the enemy very busy discouraging believers; this did not disturb me, because I had gone with an open mind and prayed much to be clearly convinced if there was anything there that did not reveal the Glory of God that I would at once have cleared out and protested against it, but God was with me there. But I found the full Presence and Power to restore believers and to heal the sick. My experience is that this does not take place in some kind of meetings, the reason is that, to a great measure, they do not believe in the full Gospel, and it is nothing new to me to find great leaders against tongues, and I find that, even in these times "they cannot enter in because of unbelief." I praise God for Pentecost.

On Sunday morning, October 26th, after waiting much on God, I went to the Salvation Army Meeting, Roker Avenue. God bless the Army. They at once gave me a welcome, and already realising His presence in my body I longed for communion, and when after praying the Glory of God covered me. I was conscious at the same time of much the experience I believe Daniel had in the 10th chapter. After this I regained strength to kneel, and continued in this Holy Glow of God all the day still realising a mightier work to follow. I went to All Saints', to the Communion Service, and after this was led on to wait in the Spirit, many things taking place in the waiting-meeting that continued to bring me to a hungry feeling for Holy Righteousness. At about 11 a.m., Tuesday morning, at all Saints' Vicarage, I asked a sister to help me to the witness of the Baptism of the Holy Ghost. She laid hands on me in the presence of a brother. The fire fell and burned in me till the Holy Spirit clearly revealed absolute purity before God. At this point she was called out of the room, and during her absence a marvellous revelation took place, my body became full of light and the Holy Presence, and in the revelation I saw an empty Cross and at the same time the Jesus I loved and adored crowned in the Glory in a Reigning Position. The glorious remembrance of these moments is beyond my expression to give – when I could not find words to express, when an irresistible Power filled me and moving my being till I found to my glorious astonishment I was speaking in other tongues clearly. After this a burning love for everybody filled my soul. I am overjoyed in giving my testimony, praying for those that fight the truth, but I am clearly given to understand that I must come out of every unbelieving element. I am already witness of signs following. Praise Him.

Smith Wigglesworth'

This experience was to have far-reaching consequences for the path of Wigglesworth's future ministry. He was forty-eight years of age when he had this experience and at that time the average life expectancy of men in Britain was only just over forty years. Many men had, by Wigglesworth's age, not only discovered their occupation in life, the majority had virtually completed their earthly course. Wigglesworth had ahead of him forty years of ministry that would take him to many places both near and far. For now, however, he returned home to Bradford to his beloved Polly, his children and the Mission in Bowland Street.

Chapter 4

A Growing Ministry

On the day that Wigglesworth was baptised in the Spirit, Alexander Boddy rushed a letter off to T.B. Barratt in Norway. The letter has been preserved in Barratt's diary, now held in Oslo.

'Oct 29 1907
All Saints Vicarage,
Monkwearmouth,
Sunderland.

My very dear Bro.,
A prominent Worker from Bradford mightily baptised today.

Glory! Mrs. Boddy laid hands on him here at the Vicarage.

So glad to hear from you (In my great haste). Please accept the small offering (£2). We can turn for thanks and prayer to God for your work and life here. Hallelujah!

In my great haste.
Alexander A. Boddy

The meetings are going on splendidly. The opportunities better but quieter.'

One year later, a 26-year-old businessman from Bourne-mouth, Stanley Howard Frodsham, was also in Sunderland. He too went to the vicarage only to find that Mr Boddy was not at home. However, Mrs Boddy laid hands on him in the same room where Smith Wigglesworth had been baptised in the Spirit just one year before and he, too, received a very powerful experience. He recalled, 'It seemed as if a thou-sand strong electric batteries came into my legs, and then a lot more came into my vocal organs – and volumes, torrents of tongues poured from my lips.' In 1910 Stanley Frodsham settled in the United States where he began his ministry in the Assemblies of God. He became a leading figure from 1916, first as General Secretary, then in the following year as Missionary Treasurer and from 1921 to 1949 as Editor of the Assemblies' newspaper *Pentecostal Evangel*. He was the author of fifteen books and, as mentioned in the Introduction, wrote the first biography of Smith Wigglesworth.

In a tribute to his old friend written for the British Assemblies of God newspaper *Redemption Tidings* following Wigglesworth's death, Frodsham related an incident connected to this story that he had heard directly from Mrs Boddy. Wigglesworth was so excited when he was baptised in the Spirit that when he got to his feet he kissed her!

One of the first things that Smith did after he was baptised in the Spirit was to send a telegraph message to his home in Bradford. Stanley Frodsham records that he wrote: 'I have received the Baptism in the Holy Ghost and have spoken in tongues.'

How did Polly react to this speaking in tongues? She had been a very effective speaker for around twenty years and, though the leaders of Bowland Street were named as

'Mr and Mrs Wigglesworth', there can be no doubt that she played the major part in the preaching.

Wigglesworth had already discovered that there were mixed reactions to the baptism in the Holy Spirit. He had become well aware of this within the ranks of the Salvation Army in Sunderland. One family, called the Tetchners, were baptised in the Spirit and went on to serve with distinction in Elim and the Assemblies of God for many years, but as far as some others were concerned it was all of the Devil! In Norway, Commissioner Samuel Logan Brengle (1860–1936) found himself in opposition to the work of T.B. Barratt, writing in one of his letters to his wife in January 1907 that General William Booth was 'fearful' of what was taking place. In Sunderland the recently arrived pastor of Bethesda Baptist Church, William Graham Scroggie (1877–1958) would also line himself up against the Pentecostals as would his predecessor, F.E. Marsh, who had been in New York and was staying in the same home as T.B. Barratt in October/November 1906. Both Dr Marsh and Reader Harris were in Sunderland during the time that Barratt was there. It was important for Smith that he should first win the sympathy and then gain the support of his wife. After that he needed to win over the members and leaders of the Bowland Street Mission.

Records indicate that Polly demanded some concrete proof and that her first reaction was to give her husband an opportunity to demonstrate this new claim of power by preaching. In a sermon published many years later, Wigglesworth recalled this event:

'I remember twenty-two years ago when I received the baptism of the Holy Ghost according to Acts 2:4, I sent home a wire (the post Office was opposite my house), that I had received the baptism of the Holy Ghost and was speaking in tongues. The news ran like wild fire – everyone seemed to know. When I arrived home my wife said to me, "So you have received the baptism of the Holy Ghost and are speaking in tongues?" She said, "I want you to know I am baptised as much as you." She said for twenty years I have been the preacher (I could not preach; I had tried many a time) … My wife said, "Next Sunday you go on to the platform by yourself – and I'll see if there is anything in it."

I had been under great pressure what I was to speak about, and as I went on to the platform Jesus said to me (Luke 4) "The Spirit of the Lord is upon thee." I don't know what I said – but my wife got up – she sat down – she got up – she sat down – she said, "That is not my husband." No man can be filled with the Holy Ghost and be the same man. He is turned into another man.'[1]

A year later, writing (with his wife's co-operation in a long letter) to Alexander Boddy, Wigglesworth reported:

'November, 1908

My dear Brother,
After twelve months of this blessed fullness I desire to witness to the truth of the anointing with power for service. There is an affinity and unity with the blessed Holy Spirit as never before, and a fearlessness, or a clothing with a consciousness that the source is His, and the results are His, and I am one channel only. It is now, without fear, a vessel unto honour for the

Master's sake. Then there is the presence of the Holy Spirit abiding – the anointing received abideth – as it is an unction from the Holy One thus renewing the spirit of our mind...

Speaking with tongues is an external evidence that God has done something, and it is always done when the motives are pure and the life cleansed ... Speaking with "tongues" brings me into a deeper sense of His abiding presence; it much resembles the Shekinah glory over the Ark. The divine glory is right over me day by day. The messages are with power; never lacking power and zeal. Of a truth God is with us. I admit that the price to pay is much, and you have to lose good friends as Elijah, but, praise God, there is a mantle of power just to meet your need.

We are getting much blessing, remarkable evidence and discernment. Faith and charity are right in this work. The mighty things will soon occur – interpretations are getting much clearer. The power of the Holy Ghost is making the dry bones feel the need...'

In a footnote Alexander Boddy added: 'We are most thankful to learn that Mr. and Mrs. Smith-Wigglesworth have recently been a blessing in the following places: Penge, Mitcham and in London at 20 Sudbourne Road, 9 Gloucester Place (W), 73 Upper Street, Islington, 14 Akerman Road, Brixton, and at Bethel Hall.'

The three last-named places are of special interest. The first, at Islington, was run by Harry Cantel and his wife Margaret, the leaders of the Zion work in Britain. The second was the home of Catherine Sophia Price (1877–1956) and her husband. Catherine was the first person in Britain to speak in tongues in January 1907 at the beginning of the Pentecostal Movement. Bethel Hall, which was the first Pentecostal church, was pastored by a Ghanaian, T. Brem Wilson, and was known as 'the black man's church'. Wilson was among the first seventeen who were baptised in the Spirit during T.B. Barratt's visit and had stayed on in Sunderland to say farewell to Barratt when he left. Boddy, in a later visit to his home accompanied by Cecil Polhill, commented on his spirituality.

As new Pentecostal meetings were established Smith Wigglesworth began to receive an increasing number of requests for his ministry. At the beginning he was sometimes accompanied by his wife. On one visit, in February/March 1909, Mr and Mrs Wigglesworth stayed for a time in Lytham in Lancashire, where former Methodist class leader Henry Mogridge was later to build a mission. A number were led into a Pentecostal experience. One night, at around 11.00 p.m. there was a knock at the door and a man in a drunken state asked to see them. They talked to him for a while asking him to sign the pledge and give his heart to God. This did not make much impression until one of the small company broke out in fervent prayer that God would convict and convert him. The Spirit began to work mightily and the man was thrown to the floor three times before he finally gave in. He was gloriously sobered up, saved and at 4.30 in the morning he went home a new man in Christ.

Stanley Frodsham tells of a remarkable story which took place in Bournemouth, where he was living at that time. Smith Wigglesworth was one of the speakers at a convention being held in the Apostolic Faith Church, Winton, Bournemouth, which ran from 26 February to 1 March. This was the first purpose-built Pentecostal church in Britain and Cecil Polhill and Wigglesworth had been there for its opening on 5 November 1908. On Sunday evening Wigglesworth preached at Winton Baptist Church at the invitation of the minister, James Brooke. Soon after, Mr Brooke joined the Pentecostal church and later became a missionary in South Africa before serving as General Secretary of the United Apostolic Faith Church.

A 27-year-old man from Birmingham, Frank Trevitt, who was suffering from tuberculosis, had been sent to Bournemouth by a specialist, Dr Lewis. He had arrived in Bournemouth on 17 February and was expected to say for six weeks. He was a very keen Christian, an active worker and a great soul winner. He was, however, in the advanced stages of TB and had not responded to treatment. Trevitt saw the meetings advertised in the local paper and decided to attend. He came to an open meeting, a weak and helpless wreck. After prayer he was baptised in the Spirit and healed. Returning his sick pay he went back to Birmingham to give his testimony. On 15 March, his doctor was able to sign a certificate of health for him and he was declared fit. Subsequently he applied to the Pentecostal Missionary Union where, after a period of training, he did sterling service in China for a number of years.

Smith was becoming well known and was in constant demand as a speaker, particularly at special meetings and conventions. These consisted of a series of meetings, usually at the holiday times of Easter, Whitsun and New Year. At one such convention held in Bradford over the Easter period 9–12 April, 1909, it was reported that between 40 and 50 people were baptised in the Spirit. The speakers on this occasion were from such diverse places as Bournemouth, London and Glasgow.

During the rest of Easter week, from Tuesday to Thursday, a Welsh Conference was held in the prestigious Park Hotel (now the Thistle Hotel), Cardiff. Amongst those taking part as speakers were the Welsh Congregational minister, T.M. Jeffreys, Cecil Polhill (who paid the expenses) and Alexander Boddy (who arrived from Sunderland on Tuesday afternoon). Mr Jeffreys reported: 'Wednesday afternoon, Bro. Wigglesworth arrived, fresh from his victories won at Bradford. His message upon the power of the Holy Ghost, was a mighty one, and brought everyone present a hunger for Pentecost. When he concluded, dozens flocked forward to definitely seek.' He went on, however, to add that 'this part of the meeting culminated in quite an unnecessary outburst of riotous emotion and extravagance, such as, if encouraged, must surely hinder the pure and blessed workings of the Holy Spirit.'

The Pentecostal Movement in Wales was in its infancy. Competent teachers were few and there were dozens of small assemblies, many of which were made up out of those 'Children of the Revival' (in Welsh *Plant y Diwygiad*). During the Cardiff meetings, when the leadership was in the hands of Boddy, Polhill or T.M. Jeffreys the more unruly elements were kept in check. When Wigglesworth was the convener of large meetings he kept things under a tight reign. At the regular Whitsun meetings in Sunderland Alexander Boddy asked those who attended to agree to obey the leading of the Chairman. It was perhaps partly as a result of reports of the Cardiff meetings that appeared in the local papers as well as in the *Daily Mail* and even the *News of the World* that the leaders were prompted to act. They had no desire to curb liberty but everything had to be done 'decently and in order'. In the report of these Cardiff meetings written by T.M. Jeffreys and published by Alexander Boddy at the end of April, the following footnote was added by Boddy:

'Sensational accounts of some of the meetings at Cardiff appear in some of the South Wales papers, in the "Daily Mail," the "News of the World," etc. We fear that the articles were founded on some scenes which may be regretted. The writers for these papers probably made the most of what they saw and heard, and naturally wrote highly interesting accounts from their point of view. We fear that what happened in some of the meetings, after we left, together with the vividly descriptive articles, will put fear into the hearts of some honest seekers, and also cause many opposers to mock. Whilst we love and respect some of our brethren very especially, we cannot approve in detail of all their methods, especially, any which seem to be efforts to work up manifestations.'

That things were not always easy nor did they always run smoothly in Bowland Street is evidenced by a report from Arthur W. Frodsham (1869–1939), eldest of the Frodsham brothers, who lived in Canada but made regular trips to Britain.

'The work at Bradford can be described as going through a period of transition. Bowland Street Mission is an old-established mission with a good record – souls saved and bodies healed, but now an element of opposition. Brother Wigglesworth is a faithful, hard worker, and is praying that those who do not see the Baptism of the Holy Ghost may be won over. He is ably seconded by his wife. They have a fine brass band, the members do good open-air work. This is a splendid feature of the work. They are not in sympathy as a body with Pentecost, and personally one feels that they may be a source of weakness in meetings. Things were conducted orderly, and the absence of the rapid repeating of a word was a good sign. The brethren need our prayers.'

From Bradford Mr Frodsham went on to nearby Leeds where he seems to have been more impressed, and he urged that the two groups should seek to get together more.

In the March 1910 issue of the newspaper the following note was inserted along with the announcement of special Easter meetings:

'S. Wigglesworth, 70 Victor Road, Bradford, Yorks.

Brother Smith Wigglesworth also requests us to insert the following: –

"The Editor regrets that in last month's issue, expressions occurred as to Bowland Street Mission which the leader feels should be re-adjusted. They admit that nothing remarkable transpired while the correspondent was there. Since then many have been Baptised according to Acts 2:4 and in every case they pleaded the Precious Blood as led by the Holy Spirit.

The Leader reports that they are in true sympathy with all Pentecostal work that is according to Scripture. Acts 2:38." '

The report of the Easter meetings was written by Thomas Myerscough of Preston and was positive. The speakers included T. Brem Wilson from London as well as several ministers from Scotland. Seventeen people were baptised by total immersion and amongst many seekers about forty were baptised in the Spirit. Mr Myerscough added:

'The harmony of the meetings was truly "one accord," and love and fellowship amongst the brethren was a great joy to my heart. It is also a great pleasure to me to record that in the meetings there was a sense of the presence of Godly control, and never did I see or hear anything to offend or hurt the most sensitive onlooker. Praise God.'

Smith Wigglesworth went on developing his ministry within the Bowland Street Mission as demands for his ministry increased from small Pentecostal missions and a growing number of conventions. It was becoming increasingly clear that his ministry should be released for the wider benefit of the worldwide Church. This would, however, be brought about not by one single act but by several factors. Some were tragic, involving the death of loved ones, while others were brought about by human error or even mischievous intent. Through it all the ministry of the Bradford plumber would encompass the globe.

Note

1. Extract from *Redemption Tidings* entitled 'The Given Glory', February 1931, pp. 6–7, quoted in Roberts Liardon, *Smith Wigglesworth: The Complete Collection of His Life and Teaching* (Tulsa, Oklahoma, USA: Albury Publishing, 1996), pp. 727–30.

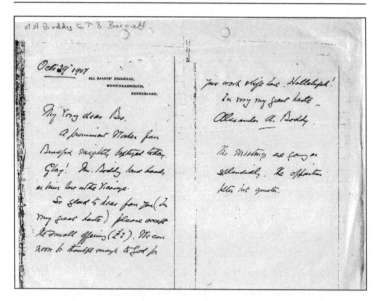

Letter from A.A. Boddy to T.B. Barratt, 29 October 1907

Smith Wigglesworth with his daughter, Alice, circa 1927

Chapter 5

More of God's Power

These were years of great joy for Smith Wigglesworth and his family. It was a source of much happiness for him to know that he and his wife were united together in purpose. His daughter Alice was a worker with the Angola Mission in West Africa, and, together with two others from the society, she was baptised in the Spirit during a 'Devotional Convention' in Preston in March 1911. Alice returned to Angola where she married Mr Smith, who was serving with the Bible Society. Tragically, as was the case with so many workers in Africa, which became known as the 'White Man's Grave', he died shortly afterwards. Later, in 1919, she married James Salter who, with W.F.P. Burton, founded what became known as the Congo Evangelistic Mission. The secretary of the Angola Mission, Miss Johnson, was also baptised in the Spirit while attending the 1911 Bradford Easter Convention. She was able to testify to her experience during the Sunderland meetings a few weeks later.

Smith continued to grow in spiritual stature and his ministry developed, particularly in the area of healing. At the Sunderland Convention, on Thursday 8 June 1911, he related the story of something that had happened to him in the town a year before.

'I was in Sunderland last year and was walking down the street with a friend when we came upon a drunken man. We said, "Will you come into our home and give your heart to God?" But the man was not willing in any way. Just then the power of the Holy Ghost showed me the way, and I laid my hands on the sinner and he could not understand the cry to God, and he came in and got saved in the house.

I was very impressed with the whole and I think it will be an inspiration to some here to know what happened the next Sunday night. The next Sunday night at our mission there was a man who was obstinate near the door; we spoke to him, but he took no notice. The Holy Ghost came and travailed with me again, and I laid hands on him, and he was convicted of sin; in less than three minutes he was crying to God at the repentance form. It may seem to some of you a very ridiculous thing to do, but I believe the power of God comes from on high.'

In March 1912, Mr Boddy was able to write of Wigglesworth's visit to Sunderland:

'We have been greatly stimulated this month by a visit of our Brother Mr. Smith Wigglesworth, from Bradford ... We rejoice to see the ripening power of the Holy Ghost in our Brother, who has truly advanced from "faith to faith," and from strength to strength ...

On Sunday afternoon and evening he gave us most helpful addresses on the **power** of the Holy Ghost coming upon us in the Baptism. Though he had known and experienced very much of the power of the Holy Spirit before he received the fullness, he knew now what a marvellous difference in power had come upon him since he received the Pentecostal blessing with the evidence of tongues.'

Wigglesworth had an impressive testimony of God's healing power in his life. Not only had he been raised from the gates of death as a young man and for fifteen years had enjoyed an unbroken record of God's healing, at the Fifth Convention in Sunderland at the end of May 1912 he spoke of his more recent experience. Wigglesworth explained that he had been suffering from appendicitis for several weeks, until eventually he was confined to his bed. Only when his condition was far advanced was the doctor called and he insisted that the sick man's only hope was an urgent operation. Almost as soon as the doctor left, two visitors arrived; one of them, a young man, came up the stairs in a big hurry. Handling the helpless man, according to his own testimony 'very roughly', the enthusiastic but unnamed young man said in a commanding voice, 'Come out, thou demon! Come out of this man.' Wigglesworth declared that 'at that instant the demon did come out and I was perfectly well, that instant, so well that I got up and went out.' The doctor returned while he was out. On hearing that the patient was not at home, he retorted, 'They will bring him back a corpse.' 'But,' continued Wigglesworth, 'it has never touched me since.' He went on to say, however, that afterwards he suffered badly from another complaint (gallstones) and did not have enough faith to trust God to heal him. One afternoon, while he was speaking to God, the power of God fell on him and he was cured. 'Would not the stones cry out against me,' he asked, 'if I did not glorify God?'

The connection between sickness and demons and the question in particular of whether or not a Christian can be demon possessed is a controversial one. It was just around this time that Mrs Jessie Penn-Lewis, allegedly in collaboration with Evan Roberts,[1] published her book *War on the Saints*. Alexander Boddy had been in regular contact by letter with Mrs Penn-Lewis. When the book was published he wrote strongly against it, warning his readers of its dangerous teaching. Though this book is still in print, its subsequent publishers removed certain passages because they did not believe that true believers could be demon possessed.

While we are on this subject it is worth noting that in the April 1913 issue of Boddy's paper, *Confidence*, there was a report written by an unnamed churchman (very possibly Rev. Thomas Hackett, a highly respected Church of Ireland minister, who was brother-in-law to the Primate of All Ireland). The author of the report made a number of favourable observations on the content and the conducting of the services (he noted in particular the way that Wigglesworth presided) during the five days of meetings that were held over the Easter holidays. Boddy, who gave great freedom of expression to his writers, left in Hackett's comments on the conduct of some of the 'helpers', who gave assistance when the sick came forward for healing. Here is an extract from his report, with some editorial comment from Alexander Boddy:

'One pleasing feature of the Convention was that the Gift of Tongues was not vainly paraded. Keen Bible students may have taken exception to the methods adopted by the helpers when dear ones knelt at the front for healing. It is unscriptural to treat any patient as if he had a demon. James 5 does not advocate it. When the sufferer is saved, and is kneeling before the Lord in faith, what saith the Scriptures of that faithful child: 1 John 5:18 "He that is begotten of God keepeth himself, and that wicked one toucheth him not."

It is grieving to see a brother act as if the wicked one had touched, when the Bible says "n-o-t". Deuteronomy 28:15 onward tells us that sickness is not an operation of the enemy. Hebrews 12:6–8 also tells how God deals with His children. Many works of grace have begun on a sick-bed – works that no demon could accomplish. These remarks are not directed to any particular visitor to Bradford, but in general to those who ascribe righteous chastisement to the enemy. May the Lord remind us each daily that the life of the redeemed is hid with Christ in God – hid from the enemy of souls. Taking the Convention as a whole, there were many seasons of prayer, praise and song. The Lord Jesus Christ was exalted as the supreme gift of God. Brother Wigglesworth was beautifully in the Spirit, souls received blessings, and hands and hearts were drawn together with strong chords of good fellowship and brotherly love.'

The editor commented:

'The Lord Jesus "rebuked" the fever in the case of Peter's wife's mother (Luke 4:38), and Acts 10:38 tells how Jesus healed all that were oppressed of the devil. In John 5:18 the touch is more of a "laying hold of" (so Westcott). The enemy cannot "get" us when we are born of God, but may attack. It is surely not "possession" by demons, but rather obsession. The evil is from the outside. Then sometimes it is God's permission (remember Job), and sometimes he is "teaching by chastisement". Hebrews 12:6–8.'

On 2 October 1912 Wigglesworth travelled to London where he was amongst the leaders and friends who were present at the dedication of Maranatha Missionary Guesthouse at 73 Highbury New Park, opened by the widow of Harry Eugene Cantel who had died a couple of years earlier. Thus he was introduced to more of this growing circle, among them Donald Gee who was baptised in the Spirit there. In later years his name appears regularly in the Visitors' Book which has been preserved.

Note

1. The word 'allegedly' is deliberate. The evidence, based upon a large collection of Mrs Penn-Lewis's letters and papers, now housed in the Donald Gee Centre for Pentecostal and Charismatic Research, show very clearly that for some time she had what almost amounted to an obsession with the activity, or alleged activity, of demons.

Chapter 6

Great Sorrow

At the close of 1912 Wigglesworth was at Swansea and Morriston in South Wales for meetings. He returned home to Bradford prior to travelling on to Glasgow in Scotland where he was booked for special New Year services. It was right at the beginning of the new year that an incident occurred that he later admitted hit him harder than anything that ever happened during his long life. The event which brought him such great sorrow was the sudden and unexpected death of his beloved wife Mary Jane on Wednesday 1 January 1913. She was fifty-two years of age. They had been married for over thirty years.

Wigglesworth owed so much to his wife's help. She had taught him to read (though he read very little apart from the Bible) and to write. In a period of extreme business in his work as a plumber during a spell of severe weather, he began to grow slack in his spiritual life. It was his wife's prayers, and her wise, tactful words that brought him back on the right path. She encouraged him when he began to preach. She kept a good home and selflessly looked after their family without complaining when he began to respond to growing calls from all over the country. If there ever was a person who qualified for the epitaph of the 'virtuous woman' depicted by the author of Proverbs (31:10ff.), Mary Jane was such a woman. Now she was dead. Such a sudden and totally unexpected loss is hard for anyone to bear. Only those who have suffered in this way can really understand the inner grief and pain. In Wigglesworth's case, however, it was in some ways doubly difficult. Here he was, a man of great faith who had clearly seen, even at this time, miracles of healing as he had prayed for people on the point of death, if not beyond. Yet now he was confronted with the enormity of such a loss right, so to speak, on his own doorstep. At first he found it difficult to accept, attempting, even at this stage, to turn back the tide.

There is more than one account of the sequence of events surrounding Mary Jane's death and, at this distance from the event, it is hard to piece together exactly what happened. One version is that Wigglesworth was at the railway station waiting for a train to Scotland when news was brought to him that his wife had died in the street on her way home after preaching at Bowland Street Mission. Another account places him still at home about to leave for the station when a policeman and doctor broke the news to him that she had died of heart failure. According to this account she had fallen dead on the doorstep of the Mission. Other variations add the detail that, refusing to accept what had happened, he addressed the apparently lifeless body, commanding death to yield its captive. According to this record, she opened her eyes and addressed him with the words, 'Smith, the Lord wants me,' to which he replied, 'My darling, if the Lord wants you, I will not hold you.'

Alexander Boddy, who had recently returned from a visit to the United States, was himself ministering in Stirling in Scotland, where he was working alongside Thomas

Myerscough of Preston, Cecil Polhill, Frank Bartleman and Mrs Polman from Holland. He carried the news of Mrs Wigglesworth's death in the January issue of his paper:

'We have to record the homecall of three well-known Pentecostal workers. Mrs Smith Wigglesworth died suddenly at Bradford (Yorkshire), on January 1st, much lamented by her dear ones.'

The others were Minnie Abrams and Mrs Murray (Bombay). It is an indication of how swiftly the news of Mrs Wigglesworth's death travelled that the same January issue carried a note from Smith Wigglesworth:

'Brother Smith Wigglesworth asks us to convey his grateful thanks to all who have written to him in this time of bereavement. He has been deeply touched.'

It says something for the calibre and strength of Wigglesworth that he was able to convene the meetings at Bowland Street for the first time in the absence of his wife for the 1913 Easter Convention at Bradford.

A further insight into the events of that tragic year is gained from an incident that brought Wigglesworth into the limelight with national press coverage. The evangelist had been participating at Alexander Boddy's Convention in Sunderland in May, where he had been one of the many speakers. George Jeffreys, the young Welsh evangelist who was to go on to found the Elim Church in Ireland two years later, was booked to continue for two weeks' special meetings. Wigglesworth, who delighted in every opportunity to minister, whether in church halls or out of doors, conducted a public open-air baptismal service in the sea at Roker, in Alexander Boddy's parish. Such an event, as good as it was, must have been highly embarrassing for Mr Boddy. The situation was given greater publicity when a report, accompanied with a full front page containing four pictures, appeared in the *Daily Mirror* on Friday 16 May, 1913. The inside story carried the headline: 'Converts' Icy Bath'. Five converts, three women and two men, were baptised early on a cold Thursday morning in the North Sea. The women, who were immersed first, were not named. The water was so cold that two of them almost collapsed from shock. The two men, both from Gateshead, were Tom James, who was described as a big silent man, and Tom Knight, a tall youth who wore what seems to have been pale blue pyjamas for the baptism. Years later, Tom H. Knight (1880–1946) would become a minister with the British Assemblies of God. His son, J.R., was a minister with the Elim Pentecostal Church for thirty years; his daughter married Fred B. Phillips, manager of the Elim Publishing Company.

Tactfully, Alexander Boddy made no reference to these baptisms in his paper and remained on very friendly terms with Smith. He would continue to give space to reports of Wigglesworth's meetings and to publish his sermons for many years to come.

Chapter 7

Great Blessing in North America

We have already traced the beginnings of modern Pente-costalism in the United States of America. Several American preachers had visited Sunderland, including Levi Lupton, Daniel Awrey and Frank Bartleman (who was there in 1910 and 1913). Alexander Boddy had been to America many times. During the years before his Pentecostal experience he had made five trips, writing the first of his travel books (published in 1896) about one of these journeys. He spent some time there in 1909 and between August and October 1912 he covered the area from Canada to New Mexico. That trip had included a visit to Azusa Street where he met Mrs Seymour.

It may have been something that Boddy had said, or a casual remark by one of the American visitors, or it could just have been that Wigglesworth needed to get away for a break and a change of scenery: whatever it was, a note inserted in the May 1914 issue of *Confidence* records:

'Our brother Smith Wigglesworth reports that his Easter Convention was well attended, and that there was much blessing. This is also corroborated by others. He is sailing for Canada and U.S.A. on April 19th, and will, we are sure, bring with him to all the assemblies he visits, the atmosphere of exultant faith, and loyalty to God's word. The story of his experiences in Divine Healing is the most stimulating and moving recital of triumphs of grace one has listened to. We commend him to the friends across the Atlantic. It does one good to hear the message from this dear Yorkshire tongue. He hails from Bradford, and his Mission at Bowland Street will surely miss him greatly.'

The home of Pastor Fisher, Lippincott Street, Toronto, was given as a contact address.

In June Wigglesworth was able to report great blessings in meetings at Montreal and Ottawa in Canada, as well as in Rochester, New York. He spoke of being warmly welcomed in all of these places. Winston Churchill (whose wife Clementine was an American) once commented that England and America were two countries divided by a common language. This set me thinking about what those first American listeners would have made of Wigglesworth's accent. The accent may have been different, but the message was always clear.

During this time Alexander Boddy made another trip to the United States and Canada, having on this occasion been engaged as chaplain on the *Empress of Ireland*. Many of the passengers on this ship were delegates to the International Congress of the Salvation Army that was to be held at the Royal Albert Hall, London, under the leadership of General Bramwell Booth. Tragically, on the outward journey, the ship had struck rocks in bad weather in the St Lawrence River and over 500 people had lost their lives, among them 148 Salvationists. Before sailing on the return ship (another vessel had to be employed) Boddy, accompanied by Cecil Polhill, attended the Memorial Service in the Royal Albert Hall. He sailed from Liverpool on 12 June and did not return until 22 August. Little did either of them know that they had been to their last Sunderland Convention. War would soon break out, with the most terrible consequences.

Perhaps, Wigglesworth thought, as many British people did, that with her standing army of 200,000 trained soldiers and a war record stretching back hundreds of years, in which they always ended up on the winning side, that 'It would be over by Christmas.' Tragically that was not to be the case. War was declared between Britain and Germany on 4 August 1914, while both Wigglesworth and Boddy were still in the United States.

In September Boddy wrote:

'Our Brother Wigglesworth tells us of great blessing at the various places he has visited. The power and unction of the Holy Spirit rests upon him as he preaches the Word of God. The Lord is with him and confirms the Word with signs following in remarkable manner. Many receive the baptism of the Holy Spirit and many are healed.

He will be in New Mexico till October, then visiting Winnipeg, Chicago, Cleveland, Toronto, Rochester, Philadelphia and New York, if the Lord tarries.'

Fortunately, Boddy wrote a detailed account of his travels and kept up a regular correspondence with many of his friends, including Wigglesworth who wrote to him at the beginning of October to say he was staying with Samuel P. Mead in Los Angeles where each afternoon he spoke to large crowds in meetings on Main Street.

Boddy's main reason for being in the States was to be one of the speakers at large camp meetings that were to be held in Cazadero, California, a beautiful site among the giant redwood trees. After an 85-mile train journey from San Francisco he arrived to find, among the crowds at the station waiting to meet him, his friend Smith Wigglesworth. Wigglesworth was the first to embrace him, followed by Stanley Frodsham. George and Carrie Judd Montgomery and George B. Studd were also there to greet him. Boddy reported in his newspaper:

'Brother Wigglesworth was like a victorious warrior, and all were thanking God for his ministry both in the word and in healing the sick, etc. Some thought he was as much used as any in this latter time.'

Describing the meetings he wrote:

'The scenes at the evening meetings were sometimes almost amazing. The people in this land are so responsive, and when a stirring address was ended they flung themselves on their knees round the platform. The whole meeting seemed to rush to the "altar," general prayer went up all over the gathering, there was strong crying often merging with praise. Then the Heavenly Anthem till all arms went up and nearly every throat was thrilling with melodious notes, and then all were next on their feet raising higher the forest of uplifted arms and upturned faces radiant under the bright light of the lamps.

The singing was hilariously joyful at times. The chorus

On the Resurrection Morning
We shall rise, we shall rise

made the assembly rise to its feet, and made all their arms and hands rise towards the skies. The dear old ladies and younger ones began to step out in the straw, and in a dignified but joyful way there was rhythmic movement of the limbs till it was almost, if not quite, what we should call stately dancing.' [1]

As the meetings drew to a close the speakers took their leave of each other. The Mongomereys prayed for Mr Boddy that he would be preserved from the dangers of warships and mines as he made his way back home to his Sunderland flock. Smith Wigglesworth embraced him on the platform of the station just before the train took him off on his long journey. Boddy asked him to keep in touch and to send him reports of his meetings for his paper.

Writing from the Great Northern Railway at Glacier Park Station on Tuesday 24 November 1914, Smith gives details of some of his experiences:

'My most precious Brother Boddy,

Your request to me, to send some reports for your valuable paper from time to time, has never slipped my memory.

I now have a dear English brother accompanying me on this trip. He, owning to reading a copy of "Confidence," was led to visit Bro. Mead in Los Angeles. He has just come from Mexico, and is in need of spiritual help. I was staying at Bro. Mead's at the time, and, being fresh from England, was soon become closely associated. This led to his baptism, and now he is most anxious to please God in any way, and is now writing this letter from me for your paper "Confidence."

I must have seen not less than 1,500 people healed and great numbers baptised into the Holy Spirit since I came into this country. My ministry, as in England, grows rapidly, and the great cry is "Do not leave us!" I have heard this cry at every place, only California's cry has been louder than that in other places I have visited.

I am now going to describe one or two things which may be helpful and useful for your paper, for they prove that the baptism in the Holy Spirit is given in accordance with Mark 16:17–18.

"And these signs shall follow them that believe; in my name shall they cast out devils; they shall speak with new tongues; they shall take up serpents; and if they drink any deadly thing it shall not hurt them; they shall lay hands on the sick and they shall recover."

The Baptism of the Holy Ghost was also clearly revealed to our minds, the gifts being in evidence, according to the 12th, 13th and 14th chapters of First Corinthians.

At all points, at all places, including Oakland and Los Angeles, the buildings were thickly packed with people eager to hear the Word of God, and one feels now, as never before, that as the Spirit rests upon us, they **press** to hear the Word of God, as is mentioned in Luke 5:1 God help me!

It was common to see, at the end of the meeting, crowds waiting for the ministry of the health in Christ, and, as in the days of the Acts of the Apostles, as one laid hands on the needy, marvellous changes were instantly wrought.

For instance, at Victoria Hall there came a woman pressed down with cancer of the breast. She was anointed with oil, according to God's Word. I laid hands on the cancer, cast out the demon, and the cancer which had up to then been bleeding dried up. She received a deep impression through the Spirit that the work had been done, and closely watched the healing process with a lady friend. The cancer began to move from its seat, and in five days dropped out entirely into the protecting bandage. They were much interested and full of joy, and, looking to the cavity whence the tumour had come, they saw to their amazement and surprise that not one drop of blood had been shed at the separation of the cancer. The cavity was sufficiently large to receive a small cup and they noticed that the sides were of a beautiful reddish hue. During the next two days, while they were watching closely they saw the cavity fill up with flesh and a skin formed over it, so that at last there was only a slight scar. At two meetings this lady, filled with enthusiasm, held in her hand a glass vessel containing the cancer, and declared how great, great things God had done for her.

This is not the only cure I could describe on the cancer line. I will give you others in a further letter.

There is a point well worth the notice of the readers of your valuable paper. At Oakland a fine-looking young man, a slave to alcohol and nicotine, came along with his wife to see if I could heal him. They stated his case, and I said, "Yes, I can heal you in Jesus' Name." I told him to put out his tongue, and I cursed the demon power of alcohol and also cast out the demon power of nicotine. The man knew that he was free. He afterwards became an earnest seeker and within 24 hours was baptised with the Holy Spirit, thus clearly confirming Mark 16:17: "In my name they shall cast out devils."

A preacher, suffering for many days from the kick of a horse, walking with great pain and in much distress, made a special call at the hotel in which I was staying, and being led by the Spirit, according to God's Word, I laid hands on the bruised ankle. A fire broke out with burning and healing power, and from that moment he could walk easily and without pain.

A boy came to the meeting on crutches, suffering from a broken ankle. Prayer was made and hands laid upon him, and I got him to walk across the platform. He declared that he had no pain, that it had gone, and carried off his crutches under his arm.

At the Los Angeles meeting all descriptions of sickness, lameness, deafness, tumours, cancers, and brokenness of spirit etc., were healed.

Truly one could say that the invitation Jesus gave was fulfilled: "Come unto me all ye that labour and are heavy laden and I will give you rest."

I notice in your paper you say that I hoped to be home by Christmas. Beyond measure I have been pressed out for duties of preaching and for Conventions, so I cannot be home by that time. If, however, the seas are free and danger removed, I would strike for home after Rochester January Convention, in order to have my own Convention at Easter in Bradford. Thus I hope to wire you so as to allow time for making it known.

I will send a fuller report the next time I write.

God bless you all and the dear saints in England, especially your dear wife.

Yours in His Name and service,
Smith Wigglesworth.'   *(reproduced exactly as written)*

Note

1. We are pleased to publish for the first time these detailed descriptions of the meetings, particularly as they are penned by a man who was not only a careful observer and a very good reporter, but also a brother much beloved. They come from his own paper, *Confidence*, which was issued from Sunderland between April 1908 and 1926. In the copy that lies on my desk, an unknown person had marked some of the above section, evidently with critical intent. It is perhaps worth stating that amongst the Jessie Penn-Lewis papers, which only came to light about three years ago, was a run of this paper as well as a number of other early Pentecostal periodicals from Britain and America. These papers (in the Penn-Lewis collection) were used by the controversial Brethren writer, G.H. Lang, in a pamphlet that he wrote against the Pentecostal Movement, with the title *The Early Years of the Tongues Movement*. He would not admit, however, being a good brother, that a lady had taught him anything.

Menston's first Wesleyan Chapel, built in 1826. The original building had stone roof slates and was described as a 'galleried box'.

Chapter 8

Wartime

It became clear very quickly, that this war, the first to be fought under modern conditions, would be both protracted and difficult, not only for the combatants but for civilians as well. In the January issue of *Confidence* in 1915 Alexander Boddy reported the shelling of his own parish which resulted in both the church and his home being damaged. One hundred people were killed, mainly women and children, in the bombardment by three enemy battleships.

The reaction to the war on the part of Pentecostals was mixed. Some like Boddy, though expressing his regret at the turn of events (he had visited Germany and had entertained many German ministers at his conferences), nevertheless expressed his support for the British action. Later, he spent a period in France as a chaplain. His only son served in the army, later transferring to the Royal Flying Corps when he was shot down. He survived but lost a leg and had to undergo many operations, from which he took a long time to recover. One of the German Pentecostal leaders, Jonathan Paul, lost two of his sons in the conflict.

Other prominent leaders, such as Arthur Sydney Booth Clibborn (1855–1939), whose wife Catherine was daughter of William Booth, founder of the Salvation Army, took a very strong line against the conflict. He republished an earlier book he had written against the Franco-German War and the Boer War entitled *Blood Against Blood*.

The immediate impact of the war as far as Christian work was concerned was that it largely limited if not curtailed much activity. Previously ordered patterns of life were disrupted. Large meetings and conventions were restricted. Young men and women were called up to register, particularly after 1916. Some of the young men who were beginning to emerge as future leaders were either sent off to fight or, in the case of conscientious objectors, were sent to work on farms or imprisoned.

In the meantime Smith Wigglesworth remained in the United States where there were still constant calls for his ministry. Alexander Boddy had not heard from him for a while and, not knowing how to get in touch with him, resorted to inserting a note in his paper:

'Smith Wigglesworth is still in the U.S.A., but we have not had any central address to which friends may always write. If he sees "Confidence" and reads the paragraph, perhaps he will kindly send us a permanent address. Mademoiselle Biolley, of the Ruban Blue, Havre, France would like him to return via Havre and hold meetings.'

Wigglesworth would eventually go and make that call but not until 1920, and again in 1921, when the war was over. Helen Biolley (*c.* 1854–1957) ran a Christian temperance hotel in Le Havre from 1896. Alexander Boddy had visited there in 1909.

Wigglesworth responded to Boddy's request, giving his address as care of Robert Pearce, 322 South 5th Street,

Darby, PA. He told Boddy that he had preached at conventions in Rochester, New York and Newark, New Jersey, and went on to say that it would be some time before he returned to England. He had had very many wonderful experiences in America.

Further American experiences

'According to promise I am now sending you my second letter for "Confidence," trusting that God will use these remarks for the furtherance of His kingdom, and the strengthening of faith of those in Pentecost.

There was much pressure brought by Mr. Moody, of Winnipeg, to leave for California for their Convention, and on the way I stopped at Portland and had a wonderful time of ministry amongst the sick. Mr. Trotter, the head of the work, wrote me a letter after my departure to say that it had been the best day they ever remember in baptising and healing the people, and I think that about not less than 50 received instantaneous healings during the day. This was a nice break on the way, and was a great blessing to one to know that the presence of God was resting upon one so remarkably. Winnipeg was also a large open door for the ministry of faith. The people gathered from far distances, and from the commencement to the finish of the Convention, which lasted for ten days, there was marked blessing.

I will now give you a few things which took place:

In one of the meetings a girl came up and said she had been unable to smell for five years, and I said to her, "You will smell today," and in the next meeting she came to testify of being healed, and I called her on to the platform, and she made a clear statement of receiving healing and smelling. Then at the close of that meeting one came up who had not smelt for twelve years and another for twenty years. I said to them, "You will smell tonight." This sounds like presumption, and certainly is extravagance of language, and on the natural lines could not be understood, but God's Word has creative power, and only in faith of the Word being creative power can we ever expect to see mighty works made manifest (Romans 4:16). "Therefore it is of faith that it might be by grace."

This is the plan which God has put into operation. If I will open the door of my heart and believe His Word, then it gives Him the power to work His Sovereign grace, and His Word becomes creative in the measure that I give Him the chance to operate by His divine power, and on the authority of His Word quicken even that which is dead, in that sense I am to believe that everything is possible. So in the name of Jesus I anointed, laid hands, and commanded the bound to be loosed, and instantly these two women were made to smell the oil. The one that had been bound for twenty years was quite an inspiration by her testimony, as she imparted faith to others by saying she had more pleasure in smelling things on the table than in eating. I cannot stop to give you all the cases, but at this place there were many wonderful deliverances.

One case more. A young woman, through many operations, had parts of her hearing senses removed from the head, and asked if that would make any difference to her being made to hear, and knowing that her faith in the Word of God could recreate the defective parts, I at once ministered according to

God's Word, believing that instant power would be given. To show that there is a necessity of the one who received to believe as well as the one who ministers to bring about God's divine plan, she left the platform as she came on apparently no different, but being in the midst of people who were constantly being defiantly healed, she appeared again the second time on the platform. She said this time, "I am going to believe that I shall be healed," and I said, "You will be healed before you leave the platform," and that night a miracle was performed. From that day she also was a great inspiration to those gathered.

A young man came to me to be delivered from nicotine poisoning through cigarettes which was wrecking his nerves, and he had tried means to be free. By faith I cast out this evil power in the Name of Jesus. Oh, if we knew the power of the Name, what it means, and how God intends to honour the simple faith in the Name.

During my ministry in Canada and the States, including New Mexico, I had got one great desire to present Jesus before the people as the great purpose in the heart of God for the relief of all mankind for spirit, soul and body. After ministering he went away. Three days after, I asked if that young man was in the meeting and there was no response – silence over the place. Then a young woman rose and said that this young man was her husband, and that the desire had all gone for cigarettes and tobacco. Glory to God.

Mr. Moody and one of his deacons kindly took me from door to door to minister to the sick, and one woman, quite hopeless and infirm, to the amazement of all in the house was made free, and began to walk up and down and praise the Lord, to the inspiration of all present. Another young man who had chronic rheumatism in his back, after being delivered he and his wife became quite penitent under the presence of the Holy Ghost.

I cannot pass St Paul (Minnesota) without giving you a description of the working power of the Spirit of God that fell upon us day after day in the assembly there. One night as the Holy Ghost fell in the healing meeting there, the joy that fell on David fell on them – they all danced and magnified God – a night long to be remembered, Glory to Jesus.

After this I called at Chicago, and great blessing rested upon me, and the healing power was mighty upon the people. Also at Philadelphia at one meeting there were over fifty people healed of all kinds of diseases, and lame leaped. Calling to see the leader at his office in one of the main streets after this, he declared that he had not been able to sleep all Sunday night through the joy of the experience of the previous meeting being so marvellous.

In my next letter I may mention Newark, Ossinning, New York City and other places.

Yours in Jesus
Smith Wigglesworth

70, Victor Road, Bradford
April 12th, 1915.'

Back in England

Despite Wigglesworth's suggestion that it would a while before he came home to England the March issue of

Confidence was able to report that he had returned and announced that he was expecting to convene the meetings in Bradford at Easter.

Alexander Boddy held his own meetings in Sunderland at Whitsun but they no longer had the same international character. There were Pentecostal meetings held in Caxton Hall, London, from 24–28 May 1915. Cecil Polhill convened the services and though the only overseas speakers were G. Polman from Holland and Archdeacon Phair from Canada, there were others from Britain, including the brothers, George and Stephen Jeffreys. Smith Wigglesworth was present at the Tuesday afternoon meeting when he 'held the people' for an hour and forty minutes. It was very unusual for him to speak for that length of time. He had a great deal to share, having returned from what he called a 'joyful sojourn' in Scotland. He told how, while he was out on a walk in Airdrie, he was able to help a brother receive the baptism of the Spirit in the open air, 'after several interruptions owing to the vigilance of the man's faithful dog.'

He also related some more of his experiences from his time in Canada and the United States. When he was in Winnipeg a man wanted his arm healed. The man said, 'I've any amount of faith, I'm simply bursting with it!' Soon he was waving his arm, and the people were greatly moved and others received healing. One of the remarks that Wigglesworth made at this time was: 'There is a great deal of difference between "difficulty" and "darkness". A man can be in difficulty all the time without being in any darkness.'

At Long Beach, California, a doctor had said, 'I am always in pain through my leg.' As Wigglesworth prayed, the presence of God drew near. He cursed the demon of pain and cast it out. 'Now,' he said, 'who do you think did it?' The doctor answered, 'Jesus.'

Wigglesworth, frequently unconventional, asked Cecil Polhill, the English country squire who was convening the meetings, to stand up. Directing the attention of the congregation to him, Wigglesworth said, 'Now look at him. God sees him as His son, not outwardly but inwardly. God wants to stir us up this afternoon to become more than conquerors through Him that loved us.' Polhill does not seem to have been offended by Wigglesworth's unusual actions. He was probably used to them by that time. If we might put it this way, you could always expect the unexpected when Wigglesworth was around. On one occasion, when he was at a meeting in the lounge of the Elim Bible College in Clapham, there were a number of ladies present who were wearing hats with very large feathers sticking out. He took a pair of scissors and, while the ladies were kneeling down, he snipped off the feathers.

In the following year Polhill and Wigglesworth would travel together for meetings that took them successively to Birmingham, Hull, Leeds, Bradford, Halifax, Hull, Lytham, Preston, Liverpool and finally to Belfast from 29 to 31 March.

Member of the PMU Council

At this time Wigglesworth was invited to join the Council of the Pentecostal Missionary Union. He met with them on a regular basis and made an important contribution to their work. Although he may not have seemed the sort of person that would really be at home on a committee, there is clear evidence from the Minute Book that he took an equal share in the proceedings. In fact, at times he was well able to argue for his sometimes alternative point of view, particularly when the discussions involved his strongly held Pentecostal convictions. At a meeting of the Council, at which Cecil Polhill presided, but neither Wigglesworth nor Alexander Boddy was present, a proposal was made regarding speaking in tongues. The relevant minute of the meeting held on 23 May 1916 read as follows:

'The question of speaking in tongues in connection with the baptism of the Holy Spirit having been considered, the Council expressed their unanimous opinion that whilst all who are now being baptised do speak with tongues, more or less, yet this is not the only evidence of this Baptism, but the recipient should give clear proof by his life and "magnify God." Acts 10:46.'

Mr Moser of Southsea was asked to draw up a formal declaration embodying the above for further consideration and confirmation by the Council. At the next meeting on 24 July, both Alexander Boddy and Smith Wigglesworth were present. They were joined by solicitor, Mr Mundell (1850–1934), the Honorary Secretary, Mrs Eleanor Crisp (1856–1923), Principal of the Women's Training Home, and Messrs Glassby and Small.

The copy of the formal Declaration which had been sent to every member of the Council having been read, it was resolved that the previous minute should be amended. It now read:

'That the Council expresses their unanimous opinion that all who are baptised in the Holy Spirit may speak in tongues as the Spirit giveth utterance, but the recipients should give clear proof of their life and "magnify God." Acts 10:46.'

This was proposed by Mr Polhill and seconded by Mr Boddy.

At a further meeting on 7 November 1916, at which the same six members were present but this time with the addition of Mr Moser, the matter was raised again. The carefully kept Minutes record:

'Mr. Wigglesworth reported that the recent decision of the Council as published in Confidence was considered very unsatisfactory by several of the Assemblies and after the Chairman had read over the draft proposed declaration of faith concerning this matter as drawn out by Mr. Moser and having outlined certain extracts of the same which it was thought might be adopted by the Council dealing with the difficulty, it was resolved that the Hon. Secretary send a copy of the extracts from the above declaration to each Member of the Council to consider and revise or adopt as might be thought advisable and that the same would be fully considered again at the next Meeting of the Council.'

That meeting took place on 5 December 1916. Neither Mr Boddy nor Mr Moser were present on this occasion. The following decision was made:

'Referring to Minute 11 of the last Council Meeting: The following declaration by the Council was unanimously agreed to:

"The Members of the P.M.U. Council hold and teach that every believer should be baptised with the

Holy Ghost and that the Scriptures shew that the Apostles regarded speaking with tongues as evidence that the Believer had been so baptised."

Each seeker for the Baptism with the Holy Ghost should therefore expect God to give him a full measure of His sanctifying Grace in his heart and also speak with tongues and magnify God as a sign and confirmation that he is truly baptised with the Holy Ghost, and the Hon. Secretary was asked to send a copy to Mr. Boddy asking him to insert the same in this month's issue of Confidence.'

As instructed, Mr Boddy published this wording. He explained that he was engaged in a mission in Northumberland at the time of the meeting and that he was therefore unable to attend. He made it clear that he fully endorsed the decision of the Council. In the same issue he also republished a Statement that had been previously drawn up in November 1909 and published in the December issue of *Confidence* in that year:

A London Declaration.
The Baptism in the Holy Ghost.

What we teach concerning the Evidence and the Results.

The sign of tongues
The "Promise of the Father" Acts 1:4 was, and is evidenced by Speaking in "Tongues" AS THE SPIRIT GIVES TO UTTER (see Acts 2:4, *Greek*; also Acts 10:46, and 19:6).

But it also includes:

Seven results.

1st. The Consciousness of the Deity of the Lord Jesus Christ (John 14:20).

2nd. The Consciousness of our "Dwelling in Him" (1 John 3:23, 24) and He is us (Ephesians 3:17).

3rd. Divine illumination concerning His Word and Will (John 14:16, 17).

4th. "The Testimony of Jesus" (Revelation 19:10; John 15, 26, 27). The Lord Jesus said that, after receiving this Promise, "Ye shall be witnesses unto Me" (Acts 1:8).

5th. The Three-fold Conviction of the Word by the Spirit in us. ("I will send the Comforter to you, and when He is come He will reprove the World of Sin, of Righteousness and of Judgment" John 16:8–11.)

1. The greatest sin of fallen man (his unbelief).
2. The need of the Righteousness of Christ (now with the Father).
3. The Judgment of the Devil (Hebrews 2:14, 15). [The Prince of the World is already condemned.]

6th. Our continual guidance into the deep things of God. (John 16:13; 1 Corinthians 2:9, 10.)

7th. The spiritual glorification of Christ (to the exclusion of self). (John 16:14; Ephesians 1:17–23; Colossians 2:15; 3:3.)'

He goes on to say:

'It is also clear from Holy Scripture (Hebrews 2:4) that God bears witness both with signs and wonders, and with divers miracles, and distributions of the Holy Ghost, according to His own will. (See also Mark 16:19, 20: John 14:11, 12.)

Gifts shall not cease.

There is no hint in Holy Scripture that the signs and miracles were to cease, or that gifts were to be withdrawn from the Body of Christ. (See 1 Corinthians 12:31, and 14:1.)

It is more than possible that the weakness and unbelief of the Christian Church is the reason for these not being more generally manifest in these latter days.

Manifestations must be for profit.

We recognise and emphasise that the gifts are for the building up (**edifying**) of the Body of Christ (Ephesians 4:7–16). We must not forget, nor allow others to forget, that the Manifestation is seen, for instance (1 Corinthians 12:8–11), in the Word of Wisdom, the Word of Knowledge, Faith, Gifts of Healings, Working of Miracles, Prophecy, Discernment of Sprits, Tongues and the Interpretation of Tongues. "But all these worketh that one and the selfsame Spirit, dividing severally to every man as He will."

Gate not goal.

It should be clearly understood that the Baptism of the Holy Ghost is the "Gate" into and not the "Goal" of a true and full Christian life.'

The original document drawn up in November 1909 was signed by thirty-one leaders representing the major figures associated with the Pentecostal Movement in Great Britain covering an area from Northern Ireland to Scotland, Wales and the Channel Isles. The purpose of the original statement was to combat the notorious so-called 'Berlin Declaration' of September 1909, which was a statement signed by fifty-six leaders from the Pietist Holiness wing within German Protestantism aimed chiefly at the teaching of Jonathan Paul (1853–1931), leader of a revivalist group who had embraced Pentecostalism in 1907. One of their main contentions was that the claims of the Pentecostals were not from on high but from below. When this Declaration was published in some of the British newspapers it caused considerable damage. None of the papers would give space to any reply, and one of the reasons for the launching of Alexander Boddy's paper was to provide a channel for reply and to present Pentecostalism in its true light.

We have no record of Wigglesworth's reaction. It is clear, however, that he and some of the leaders of the Assemblies to which he made regular visits, thought there was a danger of going soft on the more distinctive emphasis on the sign of tongues. Wigglesworth was always much more upfront than some other Pentecostals. He would regularly punctuate his preaching by breaking off and speaking in tongues and then giving an interpretation that was incorporated in the continued sermon. The early printed sermons do indicate this, but later editors of the manuscripts dropped the references to tongues, leaving only the English interpretation as part of the sermon. Wigglesworth was unique in this respect. No other Pentecostal preacher in this period followed this pattern. For this reason, some of the more staid and conservative elements were cautious about inviting him. When they did, however, it is clear that he always made a valuable contribution to their meeting and we do not hear of any complaints afterwards.

Chapter 9

Under Clouds of War

The war dragged on. The fearful slaughter on the fields of Flanders in the summer of 1916 was followed by stalemate and wearisome trench war.

Much Christian work, evangelism in particular, was severely curtailed. The emerging young evangelist, George Jeffreys, though he was sometimes engaged in preaching to troops when opportunities arose, found himself concentrating his efforts on the establishment of the Elim work in the north of Ireland from 1915 until 1921.

In Wales, the Apostolic Church emerged out of the remnants of William Oliver Hutchinson's Bournemouth-based Apostolic Faith Church. Both of these groups placed great emphasis on spoken prophecy and this resulted in increasing tension with other groups. All Pentecostals accepted that there was a place for prophecy as one of the gifts of the Spirit. The difficulty lay in the way such prophetic words were to be understood, particularly as concerned the giving of personal guidance, which sometimes had unfortunate consequences.

During the Edinburgh Conference in 1917, 'Strong feelings were expressed against "Personal Messages", owing to the havoc they had wrought. All agreed that prophecy should be on the line of 1 Corinthians 14:3: "Speak unto men, to edification, to exhortation, and comfort." This is a safe way with messages. "The others judge" 1 Corinthians 14:29.'

I mention this statement at this point for two reasons. In the first instance it is an important insight into what was being said at that time by the Pentecostal leaders meeting in conference, which is also confirmed by discussions on this same subject that were held in Sunderland, Holland and Germany. Secondly, it is important, in my view, to grasp that this is likely to have been the position with which Wigglesworth would have agreed. This becomes relevant for our understanding of what his own attitude would have been towards prophetic words that would later be attributed to him.

At the beginning of the year, Wigglesworth preached with power on 'The Inspiration of a Living Faith'. Alexander Boddy wrote to him to ask if, owing to the difficulties which could be expected under the prevailing conditions, plans were still going ahead for the Bowland Street Convention. Wigglesworth wrote in reply:

'We are quite aware of the inconveniences which will be against us in Railway Fares and Food-stuffs. But many can visit us from near centres such as Leeds, Halifax, York, Manchester, and other districts. Mrs. Crisp has promised to come, and Mrs. Walshaw, and Pastor Jeyes and Bro. Myerscough, and others, so that we shall be all right.'

An unnamed correspondent reported that the meeting proved to be a time of unusual blessing. Wigglesworth opened the meetings on Good Friday morning with a message on Acts 1:8 on the importance of the baptism of the Holy Spirit. The preaching of Christ crucified was presented as the urgent need of the heathen and the missionary offering on the Monday amounted to over £90. Another prominent feature of the meetings on this occasion was the singing in the Spirit. The writer says:

'One was very deeply impressed with the singing in the Spirit of the heavenly anthem, which far excelled anything we have had before at Bowland Street Mission. The keynote was "Worthy is the Lamb." In nearly every meeting the song was heard, rising in spiritual fervour and revelation, until it was like entering in spirit into the opening of the book of Revelation.'

At Whitsun, Wigglesworth was again one of the speakers at the convention convened in the Kingsway Hall, London, by Cecil Polhill. According to Mr Boddy he was 'overflowing'. Other speakers included Stephen Jeffreys and, for the first time, 26-year-old John Nelson Parr who was later to be a leading figure in the formation of the British Assemblies of God.

In August Wigglesworth was at Emsworth, a small village near Portsmouth where Mr D. Rodgers, editor of the local *County Express* newspaper, had established and built a Pentecostal church. Mr Rodgers had visited the Sunderland Convention and had written reports for Mr Boddy. Now Boddy was visiting his mission. He reported that Smith Wigglesworth 'had an earnest, fiery delivery, and unhesitatingly and freely used the Chairman and others on the platform to illustrate his remarkable stories.' He went on to say that this was highly entertaining to the audience and that it surely kept up their interest, as one never knew what would happen next, or whose turn it might be to be used as an object lesson. Wherever Wigglesworth ministered, or whoever else was there, everyone could be sure that things would happen. He never went in for stunts, neither did he seek to draw attention to himself. All his actions were done with a transparent honesty and an openness to the Spirit. He sought by the actions he took and the words that he uttered to bring glory to God and to create faith in his hearers. In this he was successful in spite of what some might have considered as disadvantages in his lack of education and training. In all of this he was being prepared for a wider worldwide ministry. In spite of wartime conditions Wigglesworth continued his ministry right through to the end of 1917 when he crossed over to Belfast to preach in the assembly at Hopetown Street. In the new year he was in Scotland where he was one of the speakers at the meetings in Kilsyth.

The Easter Convention in Bradford was again convened by Smith Wigglesworth and the meetings continued over a period of ten days. During that time, in spite of rationing, refreshments were provided for a total of some 2,000 people. The spiritual refreshment provided was of the highest order. Wigglesworth, in an optimistic report, expressed the opinion that he could 'see the Pentecostal features of unlimited success, when the war ceases ... clearly proving to us that Acts 2 is going on to be fulfilled in a fuller measure.' Offerings for missionary work reached a total of £200 (a considerable sum in those days – enough to buy a couple of houses in Bradford). People were said to have been baptised in the Sprit every day during the Convention. Two people were reported to have been converted and healed at the same time. At a special baptismal service twenty-seven candidates were baptised by total immersion.

Easter 1919 was to be the last occasion the Convention was held in Bowland Street. That year turned out to be the most successful financially, with the sum of £1,200 being contributed to foreign missions. Amongst the speakers were James Salter, recently returned from the Belgium Congo where he had laboured so successfully with W.F.P. Burton. Another missionary speaker, described only as Mrs Smith, was Smith Wigglesworth's widowed daughter Alice. Later that year she would marry Jimmy Salter and return with him to the Congo.

At some time, while away preaching, Wigglesworth lost control of the leadership of Bowland Street Mission. The building, which had earlier served as an educational institution, was acquired as a Memorial Hall in honour of those who had lost their lives fighting in the war. It remained in that use until 1932 when, owing to declining interest, it had to be sold to clear the owners' debts. It was purchased for £500 and became a club. It is still in use today, presently by the Catholic Knights of St Columba. The outside of the building has changed little over the years. A picture of the interior published in 1919 showed that the raised platform, over which was painted a text, 'I am the Lord that healeth thee', had been replaced by a bar.

In 1920 the Easter Convention was transferred to the Presbyterian church in Infirmary Street. The break was significant. There was a need for change. The people of Bradford, and the members and the leadership of Bowland Street had enjoyed the benefits of Smith Wigglesworth's ministry for long enough. The circumstances may not have justified the action that some of them took. As it turned out, it resulted in the building being lost and was a decisive

step in the dramatic turn of events that loosed Smith
Wigglesworth into a worldwide ministry. Such a ministry
was to make a very significant contribution to the history of
the Pentecostal Church in such diverse places as Switzerland, Sweden, South Africa, Australia and New Zealand.

Chapter 10

An Unfortunate Incident

There are several problems that challenge a writer of a biography. One problem is lack of detailed information in important areas, as well as sometimes misleading information. For anyone writing the biography of a religious man or woman, be they great or relatively unknown, there is the danger of making too much of them so that they appear to be without any weakness or failure. Such an approach is called hagiography.

On the other hand, a quite different tendency has developed, certainly since the writer Lytton Strachey (1880–1932) wrote his *Eminent Victorians* (1918), in which he was highly critical of previously revered persons such as Florence Nightingale and General Gordon. This approach rejects any writing which only focuses on the good and ignores any signs of weakness, folly or failure in the subject. Though there is much to be said for such an approach, there can be a tendency for stories only to be found interesting if there is something bad to be said about those once thought to be good. The recent phrase 'dumming down' has come to express this tendency. To quote one example, without giving either the subject or the author, a highly successful evangelist with a worldwide ministry is written off as being punished by the Almighty for the sin of pride. The evidence on which the accusation is based is no more substantial than a single remark overheard by one who ought to have known better, especially when it had more to do with the individual's own attitude towards the way the evangelist chose to dress.

An example of a successful biography is seen in the work of the writer John Pollock, especially his book on the life of Hudson Taylor, founder of The China Inland Mission, *Hudson and Maria*.[1]

The story is told of Oliver Cromwell (1599–1658) who, on seeing his portrait as first painted by the artist Sir Peter Lely, insisted, 'Mr Lely, I desire you would use all your skill to paint my picture truly like me, and not flatter me at all; but remark all those roughnesses, pimples, warts, and everything as you see me, otherwise I will never pay a farthing for it.'

When we come to discuss Smith Wigglesworth, we must come with the awareness that, though he was a great man, he was subject to the same temptations that everyone else was and is. Sometimes he could be brusque and at times he was very outspoken. He was never unkind and, if he thought that he had hurt anyone by his actions, he was quick to ask for forgiveness. He could be blunt but many of his actions sprang from deep convictions that saw most subjects in clear terms of black and white which gave not an inch in compromise on any issue.

It comes, therefore, as somewhat of a shock to discover that, suddenly, out of the blue Wigglesworth ran into considerable trouble at Bradford. The situation concerned the teaching of his friend Mr Broome, who had accompanied him on a number of his recent trips. This teaching went under the name of 'Spiritual Affinity', and involved certain men and women expressing the feeling that they had a very special relationship with each other, which was thought to be on a higher plane than mere love. It was a doctrine not dissimilar to that held by some mystical writers and, though done with the highest motives, was easily open to abuse. While the Bible says, *'To the pure all things are pure'* (Titus 1:15), it must also be remembered that *'marriage is honourable in all'* (Hebrews 13:4).

When two ladies wrote a letter of complaint against Smith Wigglesworth to Mr Polhill in October 1920, he immediately consulted with John Leech QC, a senior law officer and a member of the PMU Council. Polhill told no one else about these accusations at this stage but wrote directly to Wigglesworth to say that he regretted that he was unable to come and meet the Council and that, in his opinion, Wigglesworth ought to resign from the PMU. He went on to recommend that he should also withdraw completely from any ministry and undergo a prolonged period of rest before considering taking up any further engagements. 'We also think that you should abstain for a prolonged season from participation in the Lord's public work; and seek to retrieve your position before God and man, by a fairly long period of godly quiet living, so showing works meet for repentance.'[2]

The problem seemed to have arisen in Bradford where a meeting was called with three elders. These men concluded that the two, here unnamed ladies, had conspired together to ruin Smith Wigglesworth's ministry. Letters flowed in rapid succession. Polhill, Mundell, Moser, Boddy and John Leech were all involved. Polhill seems to have been the most insistent in calling for action to be taken against Wigglesworth. Wigglesworth complained about Polhill in a brief private note which he wrote to Mr Mundell enclosing a copy of the letter that he had sent to Mr Polhill:

'From the Letter
From Polhill He Rules
PMU & Every one Else
I think He will have trouble Later.'

The letter to Polhill reads as follows:

'My dear Brother Polhill

I duley recived your letter to day[.] I thought I would send it on to brother Mundell the Secretary as we suggested his name & Mr. Moser and Brother Boddy[.] I was thinking over the time you & Mr. Small & you had me Settling the trouble with Charley & Mr. Mrs. Small[.] You Forgave Charley & would of Forgiven Mrs. Small if she would of repented[.] I did not tell any one what I saw about to anyone[.] You could of Settled at Bradford[.] Bradford is Settled & God will settle all[.] The Good Hand of God is upon me & I will live it all down[.] This week God has rebuked the oprest thrue His Servant[.]

I shall go Forward Deer Brother and I ask you to be Careful That the Gospel is not hindered thrue you That at this time. To do unto me as you wish one to do unto you[.] do not Truble to Send any thing to Sign. I Signed my letter to you that all.

God Bless His Servants
Smith Wigglesworth'

On the reverse side of this copy which he sent to Mr Mundell he added:

'Private[.] I Pass through London on Tuesday[.] I get the 8 am train to Paris Victoria Wednesday morning[.] am thinking of Staying at the Victoria Hotel for the night if you would like an Interview I will see you no one else on Tuesday[.] I could be at Liberty After 4 o clack I think. I have one or two things to do.

Yours Faithfully
Smith Wigglesworth'

Wigglesworth was deeply upset by the nature and tone of Cecil Polhill's letter. He sent it on to Mr Mundell:

'My Dear Brother Mundell[,]

After Sending you my letter I Recived the enclosed from Mr. Polhill and I think Mr. Polhill has Steped over the Boundry this time[.] They [are] making thing[s] to appear as if I had Committed Fornication or Adultery[.] I am Innocent of thease things[.] I have done and acted folishley & God has Forgiven me[.] This thing was settled in a Scriptural way and after this at the Church & then with Mr. Polhill & he ought to of seen the thing through behind this letter to him that he will show you I will had [add] my name and Nothing Else[.]
I shall Continue to Pray for you and the Councel in General and live the who[le] thing down by the Grace of God.
God bless You

Yours in Christ Jesus
Smith Wigglesworth'

On 21 October 1920, as requested, Smith Wigglesworth sent in his resignation. In a minimum of words it simply said:

> 'I wish to resign From the Councel of The P m u
> *Smith Wigglesworth'*

In the absence of Miss Amphlett's actual letter it is not easy to decide the exact nature of her complaint. However, it is worth bearing in mind the following:

1. Wigglesworth admitted that he had been in the wrong and that he had been foolish.

2. He emphatically denied the more serious charges of fornication or adultery.

3. Because of what to us is the strange way in which ladies at that time were rarely referred to by their Christian names and were either called Miss or Mrs, we do not know which Miss Amphlett the complainant was. There were several ladies with that name. Two of them, Harriet and Sarah, who were cousins, were visitors at Mrs Margaret Cantel's home in Highbury between August and November 1915. They came from the small village of Dunhampton near Ombersley in Worcestershire.[3]

    In September 1922, when George Jeffreys was building up his work in Clapham in South-west London he sought to purchase the former Methodist church in Clapham Crescent. One of those who responded to this appeal was Harriet Amphlett, who was living at 1 Kings Avenue, Clapham. She filled in a printed card which read:

'I promise, by the help of God, to give the sum of
_____ to the Elim Pentecostal Alliance Council
towards the purchase of _____ to be used as a
Centre for the work of the Lord in _____'

In the first space she wrote, 'All she had her living.'

For George Jeffreys, it might have appeared an
answer to his prayers. However, it caused considerable
consternation. John Leech QC, President of the Elim
Pentecostal Alliance Council, strongly advised against
accepting such an offer. The lady had clearly, so to
speak, gone over the top in her action. There was no
way that they were going to take all her money and
leave her penniless. Her brother also wrote to express
his concern at such a prospect. At the end of November
George Jeffreys interviewed her and he told her that he
could not accept her offer. She was still very reluctant
to accept his refusal and wrote him a long letter. If this
was the same lady who made the accusations against
Wigglesworth, then it helps us to understand the sort
of person she was.

4.   Perhaps an even clearer picture emerges when we
consider how Alexander Boddy reacted to these events.
On 17 January 1921, writing from Switzerland,
Wigglesworth told Mr Mundell that he had received a
letter from Alexander Boddy. In his letter, Boddy had
said that he was glad that he was not present at the
meeting of the Council when Wigglesworth's resignation was discussed. It is clear that he was of the opinion
that he had been badly treated. Further proof is to be
seen in the fact that Boddy continued to keep in touch
by letter and that without any break he published
accounts of Wigglesworth's meetings in his paper.

It had been a very unfortunate incident. There can be no doubt that Wigglesworth stumbled for a time but he was able to pick himself up and continue on his way. Mr Mundell also seems to have made every effort to help. As a senior solicitor he signed papers for Wigglesworth which identified him as a 'Missionary Evangelist', thus enabling him to obtain a 10 per cent discount on his boat tickets.

Now Wigglesworth was to be engaged on a worldwide ministry that would occupy him, apart from the interruption of another war, for the rest of his life. He could indeed say, as John Wesley did, that the world was his parish.

Notes

1. Christian Focus Publications, 1996.
2. Wigglesworth to Polhill, 21 October 1920.
3. I might add that, unbeknown though this family was to me at the time, as a schoolboy I was evacuated with a family in the village of Ombersley during the war. The lady of the house was an Amphlett and her oldest son carried that name as a second Christian name. My paternal grandfather came from nearby and probably knew the family.

Chapter 11

An Open Door of Opportunity

Writing to Mr Mundell from Zurich on 6 November 1920 Wigglesworth says:

'I arrived safely and you will be pleased to hear that God had Bless[ed] all the meetings with a Broken revival Spirit and all the meetings there is rows at the Penetent Form[.] I am much Broken before God and I believe that all has Happened For my Good & so I am just walking in the light as He is in the light under the Blood[.] There is a great cry for the Missionary Field & I have had many enquiries[.] You see enemy is shut up & the people requires an open door[.] It would please you to be in these meetings[.] It is like the old time Blood and Fire days of the Salvation Army[.] There is a great Presure for longer time but I feel if I continue till Christmas it will be Good as I am not at the full strength of any Boddy.

Much love to all at your House[.] God Bless you much[.] Truly you was a Great Comfirt to me[.] Yours in His Grace[,]

His Servant Smith Wigglesworth
Faithful unto Death Whatever the Cost[.]'

(reproduced exactly as written)

His experience in Switzerland proved to be refreshing to him both in body and in spirit. Aware that there were some six weeks of hard ministry before he had a break, on 21 October he had confessed that he had been feeling tired, but gradually he was beginning to feel stronger. He wrote to Alexander Boddy who reported in the next issue of *Confidence* that Wigglesworth had spent a month in Zurich and district with further days in Bern and Geneva. The old League of Nations had been meeting in Geneva at the same time that Wigglesworth was able to report hundreds of conversions in his meetings not far away. He also wrote: 'I have seen eyes opened of those born blind, and other marvellous works done, and crowds quickened. They pressed me to promise to give most of this year to Switzerland.' In another letter he gives an account of further healings:

'A young woman was dying of consumption, and her doctors had given her up. I laid hands on her in the name of Jesus, and she knew that the disease had passed away. The girl went to the doctor, who examined her and said, "Whatever has taken place you have no consumption now."

She replied, "Doctor, I have been prayed over; can I tell the people I am healed?" And he said, "Yes, and that I could not heal you." [She then said to the doctor], "If I am to tell will you put it in black and white?" And he gave her a certificate, which I saw. God had healed her.'

There were also other cases reported:

'A man was brought into one of the meetings in a wheelchair. He could not walk except by the aid of two sticks, and even then his locomotion was very slow. I saw him in that helpless condition, and told him about Jesus. Oh, that wonderful name! Glory to God! "They shall call His name Jesus." I placed my hands upon his head and said, "In the name of Jesus thou art made whole." This helpless man cried out, "It is done, it is done, glory to God, it is done!" And he walked out of the building perfectly healed. The man who brought him in the wheelchair and the children said that, "father so-and-so is walking." Praise the Lord! He is the same yesterday, to-day and for ever.'

Wigglesworth remained in Switzerland until 7 February before going on to Norway, Sweden and Denmark for the first time. In asking for the prayers of the readers of *Confidence*, Wigglesworth described the meetings in Christiania (Oslo) with T.B. Barratt where police on horseback had to be used to control the crowds: 'So far, no buildings have been large enough, and hundreds have been turned away.' The first hall which could accommodate 3,000 proved inadequate and a larger venue with room for 5,000 had to be used. He recalled that even he had difficulty getting into the meeting place himself:

'Only by a great squeezing could I get into the hall, assisted by the police officers. Piles of crutches were left behind, the blind saw, epileptic fits were dealt with as well as many other conditions.'

He continued:

'I am at the feet of Jesus, and weep through my address, and God breaks up the people, and there are rows of people each night seeking salvation.

A poor lame man in hospital asked the doctor for leave to attend the meetings, but was refused permission. He was told that if he broke the regulations he would not be allowed to return. He replied that he did not expect that he would have to return and it was so.'

When Wigglesworth laid hands on the man (knowing nothing about what the hospital doctor had said) he was healed. He left his crutches behind.

Arriving back home in Bradford at the end of December 1920 he found many letters requesting his services. After a brief visit to Sheffield for New Year, he was home again when he received an urgent telegram from South Wales: 'Come at once the last Ray of Hope A man dying with cancer no Hope'. Wigglesworth hurried there, going via London. Describing what happened in a letter to Mr Mundell, written from Bradford on 17 January, he said, 'God raised him up and all pains left and I left him walking and eating. Many others healed of other complaints.' In the same letter he told Mr Mundell that he had left England, 'Troubled and near brokenhearted. But every day got brighter and the crowds lifted higher and higher and all the time God witnessed to me freedom and blessing.'

So it was to continue throughout the year as he moved from place to place ministering in France, Switzerland, Denmark, Norway and Sweden. Everywhere he went there were converts and many outstanding healings. Some of the churches gave generously in response to Wigglesworth's request that the offerings be given to missionary work. Throughout the year he gave regular, and sometimes substantial sums to support the overseas missions work of the PMU and the recently established Congo Evangelistic

Mission work begun by W.F.P. Burton and his son-in-law, Jimmie Salter.

With all the crowds, particularly in Switzerland and Sweden, problems arose with the authorities. In Switzerland on two occasions he was arrested by the police and lodged in a police cell. Someone, having heard he was taking up offerings at the meetings, seems to have complained that he was out to make money for himself. These offerings were expressly used to support mission work and not to encourage any elaborate lifestyle for himself nor to establish any elaborate machinery of ministry. The men who arrested him told him that they had nothing against him and that they recognised that he was doing a good work there. On one occasion they came to him in the middle of the night to release him. 'You are free to go,' they said. At first he refused. 'No,' he said, 'I will only go if every officer in here gets on his knees and I pray for you all.' One can only imagine what it would have been like to have been locked in a police cell with Smith Wigglesworth, even for one night!

The authorities perhaps feared the danger to public safety should a large crowd, even in Sweden, rush the platform when seeking to be prayed for with the laying on of hands by the evangelist. The New Testament tells the story of those who sought healing when the waters of the pool of Bethesda were disturbed. One man had been waiting there for more than thirty years and had failed many times to be the first one into the pool, presumably because others had pushed him out of the way. There would have been many an undignified scramble over the years. This man was healed after Jesus singled him out.[1] Pentecostal healing evangelists from the beginning all found it necessary to adopt some form of technique when dealing with those who came in considerable numbers to their meetings with the hope of being healed.[2] Some asked those requiring prayer to form a line after they had preached. The evangelist would invite them to come on to a raised platform where he prayed for them individually, inquiring what was wrong. After a simple prayer or sometimes the anointing with oil they were then led off the platform by an assistant. Testimonies were sometimes immediate, often causing great excitement, particularly when there was visible evidence of a cure. Later, this had to be refined in order to regulate the huge response and cards were introduced which gave space for the name and address of the sufferer and sometimes an indication of their condition, though this was not insisted on. These contact addresses were useful, particularly for the more denominational evangelists who were seeking to establish a new work or build up an existing fellowship. In some cases the details of the person's name, address and the complaint from which they had been suffering were later publicised (with their permission) by the evangelist. In outstanding cases tracts and pamphlets were also produced, sometimes with 'before' and 'after' photographs. In Wigglesworth's case he never bothered about names at all. He kept no lists. He had no mailing list as such, though he did sometimes write to those who had been healed through his ministry but this was never on a regular basis (he was far too busy for that, and perhaps not that well organised either!). He was quite content to leave them in God's good hand, though he was careful also to insist for their future spiritual and physical prosperity that they needed to be linked with a good, lively church and also keep their own spiritual life in a healthy state by a daily diet of prayer and Bible reading.

During this first visit to Sweden in April and May 1921, he ministered for Lewi Pethrus, the outstanding leader of the Swedish Pentecostal Churches. At that time this work, which was to become the largest Christian group outside of the Lutheran State Church, did not have a church building of their own. In Stockholm they met in an auditorium and in the YMCA, which made their meetings very public (which evangelistic meetings are intended to be; they were never meant to be held in secret or behind locked doors). It was through this sign-attested ministry, as it would later become known, that many were first attracted to the meetings and a good number were converted and healed. In some cases whole families were involved and the ongoing testimonies were passed on through the family to their children and grandchildren.

Such public demonstrations caused more than a few raised eyebrows. Much of the press spoke out against such goings on and in addition there was opposition from a combination of religious leaders and members of the medical profession. The outcome of this was that following a meeting of religious leaders, medical men, the police and even the king, restrictions were placed on Wigglesworth's ministry. The aspect that some found most objectionable was that he prayed for and laid hands on the sick openly in public.

A nurse who was a member of the king's household had been healed in one of the meetings and as a consequence was able to walk. When Wigglesworth shared this story with a group of students in Los Angeles in July 1927, he could not remember if she had a broken thigh or a dislocated joint.[3] The king was made aware of this healing and he expressed his sympathy with Wigglesworth. His advice was that in order to avoid any further trouble, and also to leave the door open for any future visit, Wigglesworth should simply leave the country in order to avoid being thrown out. This is in fact what happened. As he told the students: 'I thank God I was not turned out, I was escorted out.' This did not happen, however, until the final meeting had taken place on Whit Monday. In order to keep faith with the authorities and yet be able to minister to the large numbers who still needed healing, Wigglesworth adopted a new means of praying for such a large number within a minimum amount of time and with the least degree of disorder. Fixing his attention on a lady who was standing on a vantage place on a rock he asked her what the matter was. She said that she was in great pain all over. He prayed for her without leaving the elevated platform. She was instantly healed and began spontaneously to leap and dance for joy. He then asked all of those who were sick and who desired to be healed to place their own hands on the afflicted place (if this was appropriate). He then prayed and afterwards it was reported that a large number were cured. Thus in spite of the reticence of some and the active opposition of others, the ministry of this man of God was more than vindicated.

Wigglesworth's ministry was much more than that of a healer. He told those same students in 1927: 'Don't go mad on preaching healing. You will be lopsided.' In New Zealand he said that he would rather one soul was saved than ten thousand healed.

Notes

1. John 5:1–9.

2. An interesting and useful guide that tells the story of the later healing evangelists in the United States, particularly in the period between 1947 and 1958 is David E. Harrell's *All Things Are Possible* (Bloomington: Indiana State University Press, 1975).

3. Roberts Liardon, *Smith Wigglesworth Speaks to Bible Students* (Tulsa, Oklahoma: Albury Publishing Company, 1998), p. 215.

Wigglesworth's letter of resignation from PMU, 21 October 1920

Letter from Smith Wigglesworth to George Jeffreys, 3 July 1923

Chapter 12

To the Uttermost Parts of the World

In his history of the Australian Pentecostal Church Barry Chant tells us:

> 'One of the most interesting figures in Australian Pentecostal History was Smith Wigglesworth. In fact, he only visited this country twice and spent no more than two years here altogether. But in that time he made a powerful impact on the people who heard him. Many hundreds were converted and many of them were ultimately brought into the Pentecostal Movement.' [1]

Smith Wigglesworth sailed for Australia at the end of 1921, arriving there after holding meetings in Ceylon (now Sri Lanka). The invitation had come from Mrs Janet Lancaster, leader of Good News Hall, North Melbourne. Known affectionately as 'Mother' Lancaster, she was one of the pioneers of Pentecostalism in Australia. With the invitation she sent a sum of £250 which was more than enough to cover the cost of travel. Her daughter, Leila (Mrs Buchanan), took down a number of Wigglesworth's sermons and these were included in the book *Ever-Increasing Faith*, which was published by the American Assemblies of God in 1924.

The meetings began on 30 April in a Sydney Baptist church. They were arranged by Dr R.H. Fallon, a medical doctor and former Baptist minister, who went on, a few years later, to serve as a Pentecostal minister in New Zealand and in South Africa. Mr Lamb, the minister of the Baptist church where the first meetings were held, was not aware that Wigglesworth was Pentecostal before the meetings began but he soon became very quickly aware of the fact. In that first meeting there was a lady in a wheelchair. Calling her to the front of the building, Wigglesworth boldly declared:

> 'I want you folks to know that I am going to prophesy in the name of the Lord that this woman is going to walk. If that prophecy does not come to pass, I will never prophesy again. But if it does come to pass, you will know that there is a prophet in the midst.'[2]

As we can well imagine, that caught the attention of everyone. Describing the incident, Phillip Duncan, then a member of the church, said, 'All the deacons were looking at the minister; Dr Fallon was looking at his boots; Wigglesworth was looking to the Lord.' It was a most dramatic introduction for any mission. Even for Wigglesworth it was unique. One is perhaps reminded of the case of the crippled man at Lystra (Acts 14:8–10) where Paul perceived that the man, lame from birth, had faith to be healed.

Without any fuss, Wigglesworth calmly addressed the woman: 'In the name of the Lord, be free.' He then lifted her out of the chair, with the words, 'Now walk!' Obviously nervous, the woman said that she was unable to do so. Wigglesworth told her that the Lord had healed her and that she could now walk. With that, he pushed her in the middle of the back and she walked.

Some people were highly impressed. Others were appalled by his seemingly high-handed and presumptuous manner. That was the first and the last meeting in the Baptist church. The meetings moved to the Australia Hall where they continued for six weeks. Wigglesworth then travelled on to Melbourne where he held meetings in the Good News Hall. Miracles of healing followed his ministry there also. Here is just one example.

Mr Harrison was a schoolteacher. Owing to the fact that he had more than thirty cancerous lumps on his neck he was unable to wear a collar and tie. He was in constant pain which made it difficult for him even to bear the dressings on his sores. Specialists said that surgery would not help.

Harrison attended a meeting in the Good News Hall. Wigglesworth told him, 'Go home and sleep. In the morning, take the bandages off', and with that he slapped him on the back of the neck and commanded the growths to go in the name of the Lord. The next morning there was no trace of any growths at all. His son, C.C. Harrison, who later became Principal of the Commonwealth Bible College of the Australian Assemblies of God, in relating the story of his father's healing, said, 'Wigglesworth seemed rough and ready, but none ever complained. He was a man's man, and completely fearless. At the same time he could be gentle. He never said no to the sick, day or night.'

Such was the interest in the meetings that they moved to the much larger Wirth's Olympia, one-time home of a famous circus. Meetings were held daily (except Monday and Saturday) from Sunday 19 February through to 5 March.

The newspapers carried bold advertisements and large crowds came to see what was taking place. Altogether 1000 people professed conversion.

From Melbourne Wigglesworth moved on to Adelaide where miracles of healing were also in evidence, though the crowds were not as large. Many years later Mrs Watson related the story of her husband's healing as a young man. He was suffering from a very poisoned hand and was due to go into hospital the next morning. 'Well, sonny, what's up with you?' demanded Wigglesworth. When the young man explained what was wrong, the evangelist said, 'That's all right, the Lord knows all about that. Put your trust in the Lord. You'll be all right', and moved on to pray for the next person. A few minutes later he returned to the young man and said, 'Hey, sonny, take those bandages off.' When he did so, there was no sign of any swelling and no visible mark at all. He was perfectly healed.

Writing to Alexander Boddy, Wigglesworth outlined his future plans and indicated that he found himself looking forward to a rest on the week-long sea trip to New Zealand that was to be followed by a further three-week voyage to America. He wrote:

'God is doing wonders. We have meetings in a picture house, and crowds are being saved night by night. This morning a girl, 16 years old, who had been stone deaf eight years was instantly healed, and similar mercies are going on all the time. I spent Easter in Melbourne, and enclose a few testimonies from those helped there.'

He followed this with a second letter on 24 May, in which he added some more testimonies from his correspondents.

Later, also at Sydney, he said: 'This has been a great week of soul saving. Crowds are being stirred up. Ministers and preachers, many have begun a new life. The presence of God has been mighty.'

Testimonies

'107 Row Street, North Fitzroy,

I feel I must express my deep gratitude for the blessing received. Only those who have been in the furnace of affliction can realise the joy of deliverance. It seems too wonderful. After fourteen years of anguish, sleeplessness, and spiritual depression, caused by the bondage of the adversary, these are things of the past. As Bro. Wigglesworth says, consumption is of the devil, and only the Lion of the Tribe of Judah could have delivered me from this dread scourge, which had made my body a mass of corruption. Hallelujah!

Kathleen Gay.'

'Baille Street, Horsham, Victoria.

I was prayed for in Melbourne, and the evil spirit was commanded to come out. I had a polypus growth in my nose. It had been there eighteen years. When I came home from Melbourne the growth all broke up and came away, for which I praise God. I had also a pain under my left breast which had troubled me twelve years. I think it was a leakage of the heart, as sorrow had caused it in the first place. At times I used to vomit blood. I have deliverance from that also. All praise to our wonder-working Jesus.

Mrs. T. Simcock.'

'32 Emerald Street, Collingwood.

I have had [a] liver complaint all my life. When quite a girl I was treated by the best doctors, but it always returned, and at times I was unable to turn in bed without help. The last twelve months my kidneys were bad, and my legs swollen much with cramp. I had also varicose veins, with lumps larger than an egg. Now, glory to God, all has gone – disappeared – as soon as hands were laid upon me in the name of Jesus. I am hungering and thirsting after the Baptism. Please pray for me.

Catherine Rutherford.'

When, five years later, Wigglesworth returned to Australia, the magazine *Australian Evangel*, carried more than a dozen outstanding testimonies of healing from his previous visit.

From Australia he sailed to New Zealand, where he held his first meetings in Wellington, proceeding to Christchurch and Dunedin before returning to Wellington. Through some misunderstanding he had originally been expected in November 1921 and there had, in fact, even been an announcement for the opening meeting in Wellington Town Hall on Monday 21 November. The original sponsoring group was an inter-church group known as the Christian Covenantors Confederacy, which had been founded in 1919 and met every Saturday in Vivian Street Baptist Church, Wellington. The origin of the invitation to visit New Zealand was the result of a meeting between Wigglesworth and the former Danish CIM missionary, J. Fullerton, who had embraced Pentecostal teaching. The missionary had met Wigglesworth during his meetings in Denmark but he had had to return to China before Wigglesworth arrived in New Zealand.

News of what had occurred in Australia had evidently reached New Zealand. Though publicity was somewhat limited, those who came at first were hoping that similar results would obtain. They were not to be disappointed. The Baptist minister, Dr Catchpole, who had witnessed the Welsh Revival, offered his Sunday school hall, Vivian Street, for the opening meeting. On Sunday morning Wigglesworth preached at Berhampore Baptist Church on his favourite topic of faith. It was to be the first and last ordinary church service at which he ministered during the crusade. In the evenings they held meetings in the Town Hall. On the first Sunday evening there were some 800 present but by the third evening the numbers had swelled to 3,000.

One evening, almost a thousand people were unable to gain entry to the meetings. A Salvation Army officer, who had come from Brisbane to attend the meetings, stood on the steps of the Town Hall and preached the gospel to the crowd. At the end of his message he made a public appeal to which more than twenty responded. Miracles of healing were also reported.

The meetings caused a considerable stir. At the end of May the local paper, *Dominion*, carried the bold headline: 'Faith Healings, Extraordinary Scenes at Town Hall; the Deaf Made to Hear.' Many of the local papers, which carried the titles of many of the local ministers' sermons for the early Sundays in June, turned their attention to addressing questions on healing and the presence or the absence of miracles.

In an attempt to bring about a closer harmony between those conducting the mission and local ministers, Wigglesworth addressed the Wellington Council of Churches. The purpose was to bring about a better understanding of Pentecostal teaching and the phenomena which frequently accompanied it. Regrettably, but not unexpectedly, the meeting only widened the gap.

Several newspapers carried reports of the meetings. Some gave positive coverage, others were highly critical. Following an initial report on 11 June, the editor of *The Sun* penned a highly critical piece entitled 'There Are No Miracles'. It sparked considerable debate, and a number of letters, both for and against, were published over the next few days. In addition to a response from H. Roberts, the Secretary of the Wigglesworth Mission, two letters were sent in support by a barrister, John A.D. Adams (1844–1936). Mr Adams said:

> 'Mr. Wigglesworth's audiences were composed of men and women who can think and are accustomed to take an intelligent part in the affairs of life ... These people saw things done, and applauded, and thanked God for what they saw. I cannot believe they were so deluded as to think that they saw what they did not see, and what another person with no more knowledge than they, and perhaps with less experience, says did not happen. From what I myself saw and heard I have no doubt whatever that Mr. Wigglesworth's work is of God. He is on clear scriptural lines and God is blessing him and his work. I have seen things happen in these meetings which cannot be explained unless they were supernatural.'[3]

It was an impressive testimonial.

After ministering in Dunedin from 18 June until the end of the month, Wigglesworth returned to Wellington, where he opened on Sunday 2 July in the Town Hall. Such crowds came, both to the Town Hall on Sundays and to Taranaki Street Methodist Church during the week, that Wigglesworth had to ask the police to help him to get into the meeting in order to preach. According to the caretaker of the Methodist church, who was over eighty years of age, the meetings reminded him of how things were in the early days amongst the Methodists in London.

As a result of these meetings the New Zealand Evangelical Mission became the Pentecostal Church of New Zealand in 1924. Harry Roberts (1863–1949), mentioned above as the Secretary of the Wigglesworth Mission, was its first General Superintendent. He had been converted during the mission of the British evangelist, Henry Varley in Wellington in 1879 (he played for the All Blacks in 1884).

Wigglesworth returned to New Zealand in October 1923 remaining until the end of December 1924. He began in Auckland and continued there well into January. There were many converts. What had started as a mission moved on to become a convention for part of the latter period consolidating the work. Once again controversy was stirred up, this time involving Evangelicals, Brethren and Rationalists. A Baptist minister in Palmerston North announced in his sermon, 'The Tongues Movement proved to be Demoniacal' and the Rationalist, H. Scott Bennett, called it 'Theological Vaudeville'.

Generally speaking the reporters who attended Wigglesworth's meetings gave a fair assessment of what they observed. In some cases in particular we have cause to be grateful for the descriptions they provided, since the reports in the Christian papers were at best vague with hardly any real details being given. A report in the *Marlborough Express* of 10 December 1923, whilst seeking to play down the impact of the mission, provides some interesting comments on the conduct of the meetings. The article bore the heading 'Smith Wigglesworth Mission. A Wordy Evangelist'. What makes this unusual is that, whatever else can be said about Wigglesworth, he rarely preached for a long time. Very few of his published sermons, which number around 165, could be described as lengthy.[4] From comments that he made on more than one occasion he was much in favour of shorter sermons. It could be argued that, at least in his own case, because his sermons had little or no structure and because he had no notes to guide him, he would have forgotten what he had said earlier on anyway. He once told a congregation a story about a preacher who was somewhat longwinded. A brother who had heard part of the lengthy sermon had left the meeting while the preacher continued his discourse. When he got outside someone asked him, 'Has the preacher finished?' 'Yes,' the man replied. 'He finished some time ago, but he is still speaking.' The important factor for Wigglesworth was not the length of time but the content of the message. The quality of his sermons does not easily come over just by reading them. All, even the most hostile critics, had to acknowledge that there was a special 'something' when Wigglesworth was the speaker. It was this, right from the beginning, that caused a number of people to take these messages down in shorthand in an attempt to recapture the intense feeling of the time. This was almost unique at that period. Later generations had the opportunity of using mechanical means of tape recorders, microphones and video cameras to make recordings. Apart from a single film sequence, taken by an American visitor to Britain a year before his death, no other living record of Wigglesworth is known.

The *Marlborough Express* reporter said that on this occasion Wigglesworth began his discourse on the Four Square Gospel before 7.30 p.m. and was still at it at 9.00. He described the preacher as 'a big brusque Yorkshireman, who preaches a sermon like an endurance test.' He then went on to tell how, at the end of the sermon, Wigglesworth asked four people who were suffering pain to stand up and be prayed for. He then asked God to demonstrate his power by setting them free. All four claimed to have been freed from pain. One elderly lady, who had not hurried for years, ran up the aisle without difficulty.

> 'His method is rather remarkable for he stands on no ceremony. With coat removed, he "laid hands" very violently indeed on the afflicted parts of the various people's anatomy while he called in stentorian tones on the evil spirits possessing them to come out, and in one case dealt a frail old lady such a smack in the stomach as might have doubled her up. His patients, however, stood up unflinchingly to his assaults, and in every case declared themselves improved in health by the encounter.'[5]

Notes

1. Barry Chant, *Heart of Fire: The Story of Australian Pentecostalism*, second edn (Unley: Luke Publications, 1975), p. 50.

2. Ibid., p. 51.

3. *Otago Daily Times*, 24 June 1922.

4. For the largest (though not complete) collection see Roberts Liardon's *Smith Wigglesworth: The Complete Collection of His Life and Teaching* (Tulsa, Oklahoma, USA: Albury Publishing 1996).

5. *Marlborough Express*, 10 December 1923.

St. Jude's War Memorial Hall in Bowland Street, Bradford, taken in 1931

Chapter 13

Increasing Influence at Home

During the time that Wigglesworth had been circling the globe as a roving evangelist there were many changes within the Pentecostal Movement in Britain. Alexander Boddy had retired from his church in Sunderland in 1922 and moved to the small village of Pittington near Durham. He continued to edit the newspaper *Confidence* but it appeared less frequently and his involvement in the work of the Pentecostal Missionary Union declined. Eventually, in 1925, the Union was merged with the Assemblies of God of Great Britain and Ireland which was formed in Birmingham in February 1924. This new grouping was initiated when a number of churches in Wales made application to join the American Assemblies of God in 1922. A number of conferences were arranged in Sheffield, London and Birmingham before the Fellowship was brought together. Half of the seventy-eight assemblies were in Wales with the north of England also being strongly represented. Within three years the Fellowship had grown to more than 200 churches, with over sixty in Wales.

George Jeffreys had started the Elim Evangelistic Band in Ireland in 1915 and in 1921 he opened his first English church in Leigh-on-Sea, Essex. In the following year, together with his brother Stephen, he entered London where he pioneered a church in Clapham. This was followed by the first of a series of meetings in the East End that would be continued over the next ten years. As a result of these meetings the Pentecostal message was boldly proclaimed and a number of large and successful churches established. The original Apostolic Faith work of W.O. Hutchinson was much reduced in size. Most of the churches in West Wales went to form the Apostolic Church under the capable leadership of Daniel Powell Williams.

At the end of 1923 Alexander Boddy reported that Wigglesworth had once again gone off on his worldwide travels in response to an urgent call from New Zealand. This time he journeyed from East to West, stopping off to minister in assemblies in Montreal and Vancouver, British Colombia.

Though Alexander Boddy's paper now only appeared quarterly, he still continued to give reports of Wigglesworth's travels as their regular correspondence continued, and from time to time he published his sermons. For many years these had been taken down by stenographers, frequently by Mrs F.E. Braithwaite. The use of various forms of shorthand for taking down sermons has had a long history. By these means the sermons of John Calvin (1509–64) on many of the books of the Bible were preserved and the great Victorian Baptist preacher, Charles Haddon Spurgeon (1834–92) had his sermons recorded every week for many years. These were then transposed so that Spurgeon was able to edit them for publication every week when they went on sale to the public. For the sermons of a Pentecostal preacher to be given this treatment was unique. Clearly, quite early on some people must have been aware, after being in Wigglesworth's meetings and listening to him, that there was something very special taking place.

Around this time Boddy published a sermon bearing the title 'Divine Life and Divine Health', which was probably given in Canada. There is another sermon, contained in the collection published by Roberts Lairdon, which bears a similar title, 'Divine Life Brings Divine Health'. The first was based on the life of Peter and shows how his weakness was turned to power. The second, first published in Australia in 1925, had its starting point in the beginning of Mark's Gospel. The repetition evident here is quite unusual in Wigglesworth's recorded sermons. Other men, from John Wesley to Pentecostal preachers like George Jeffreys or Donald Gee, regularly repeated their sermons as they travelled from place to place. Indeed, Gee kept a detailed record of where and when each sermon was preached. Wigglesworth kept no such record. He used no notes and had no particular sermon outline. He did have regular themes, particularly on the subjects of faith and the gift of the Spirit. Here, however, there is evidence of the importance that Wigglesworth attached to teaching new converts that the power of the risen Christ was available to them to enable them to live victorious lives. One of the truths that was repeated in both messages is found in the rhetorical question, 'Do you think that God would make you to be a failure?' According to his gospel, 'God never made man to be a failure.' This was the very word that these new converts needed. He reminded them of their potential in Christ through the power of the Spirit. The message was the same, be it in Australia, New Zealand, Canada, the United States of America or back in Britain. What he began to proclaim in 1907 after he was mightily baptised in the Spirit, Wigglesworth continued to preach for the next forty years.

In 1924 Wigglesworth was given ministerial credentials by the American Assemblies of God. It was the only time he ever held any such credentials. He described himself as 'evangelist-teacher'. In some ways it could truly be said that he surely carried with him those apostolic signs and wonders that needed no other authentication (2 Corinthians 12:12). The main advantage that these official papers gave him was that they enabled him to take advantage of concessions on train fares that were available to ministers in the United States. Wigglesworth was always well dressed. He usually travelled in the better class compartments. When once someone tried to rebuke him (which not many did), accusing him of wasting the Lord's money, he replied, 'I'm not wasting the Lord's money, I'm saving the Lord's servant.'

In later years the crowds were not always as large as they had once been. One of the reasons for this was perhaps due to the timidity of some of those who invited him. Some of them seemed to want to confine his work to ministering to the saints in their little upper rooms, often in dingy back streets. But even there many wonderful things took place. In response the churches sometimes dug deep into their reserves and gave generously to support the work of oversees missions at his expressed wish. In one place, the lady in charge of the mission, received £50 a year. For a mission lasting a few days they gave Wigglesworth over £27 which he passed on to support missionary work.

The establishment of the Assemblies of God in Britain in 1924 opened up many requests for his services. In between continued trips overseas, there was rarely a Sunday that went by when he was back in Britain that did not find him preaching at some assembly or other. From 1929, after the

Elim Church was established in the city, he would be found in the service at Southend Hall. He always had a word to impart. One of the ministers who pastored there during this period told me, 'You did not have to invite him to speak, he always volunteered.' It was always brief and to the point, and it was always beneficial.

The British paper, *Redemption Tidings*, announced in its second issue of October 1924 that a book containing eighteen of Wigglesworth's sermons had been published. Later it reported that 11,000 copies had been sold and that the profits had been given to support missionary work. It also reported that Wigglesworth expected to be present for the Preston Convention in Easter 1925, along with a number of missionaries. Missionaries working with the Congo Evangelistic Mission, founded by W.F.P. Burton and James Salter in 1919 out of an earlier pioneer work, were always well represented at this convention. Wigglesworth always convened this meeting, and his son-in-law, Jimmy Salter, now Home Director of the CEM, also took a prominent part.

Apart from his regular appearances at conventions in Kingsway, London, during Whitsun, and Preston at Easter, Wigglesworth had meetings in Edinburgh, where Donald Gee was still in his first and only pastorate. The response in Scotland that August seems, however, to have been somewhat muted.

In a rare visit to North Wales where he ministered in Old Colwyn, there was a very interesting report in the *North Wales Weekly News* of 10 September 1925:

'Interest in the mission became very pronounced when bills were put up stating in bold type that the days of miracles are not ended, and that Evangelist

Smith Wigglesworth, of Bradford, proposed to prove this statement.

The meetings were held in the Y.M.C.A. on Thursday night, where there was a large crowd gathering.

The meeting was opened by Brother Parr with prayer. Revival hymns were subsequently sung with extraordinary cheerfulness and enthusiasm. Mr. Wigglesworth then discoursed on Matthew 8:1–17, dealing in particular with the cleansing of the leper and the healing of the centurion's servant by Christ.

The preacher said that the one condition of healing was belief in what God's word had said, "and I am here tonight," he added, "resting only on God's word; and if I fail in the privilege of changing or moving you, you can say as you go outside, 'God is not with him.'" He said with great emphasis that his great desire was that everybody should be saved. "Thirty-five years ago, I was a weakling, helpless, and dying, when God in a single moment healed me. I am now sixty-six and as fresh as any of you and as ready for work as I ever was. It is a wonderful thing to know that you have no indigestion, no constipation, no corns to trouble you and this is possible for you through Christ, and I am here to help you and to give the Lord the glory." The evangelist asked those present who were suffering from any ailments to stand up, and fourteen people – six males and eight females – immediately did so.'

The reporter went on to give details of some of those who were healed. One middle-aged woman with rheumatism was able, when commanded by Wigglesworth, not only to lift both of her arms but to walk and then to run. She ran down the aisle and onto the platform, much to the delight of the onlookers. An elderly man was also able to run with apparent ease after claiming to be cured of a double rupture. Several other cases were also reported. John Nelson Parr, the first General Secretary of the Assemblies of God, who had travelled over from Manchester, added a footnote:

'While the meeting was going on someone who saw the first man healed ran out and brought a man, who had lost the sight of one eye through the action of lime. This man was prayed for and declared that he could see the congregation with this eye when the other eye was covered up. A gentleman met him next day and asked him how his eye was going and his testimony was, "I can see as well with the eye which was blind as I can with the other."'

Around this time Wigglesworth also ministered in a convention in Llanelli as well as at Machen and Crosskeys in Wales.

In October 1925 he spent three days in Chesterfield where there was a small Assembly of God church. Some 200 turned up for the first meeting in the Town Hall on the Saturday and there was an even better response over the next two days. This visit was all too brief. The town, noted for its crooked spire, would have to wait for two years before Welsh Evangelist Stephen Jeffreys visited there for a three-week mission in the skating rink which really put the assembly on the map.

In the Spring of 1926 Wigglesworth left Britain to visit Ceylon, having just returned from spending two weeks in Switzerland. He reported that in Zurich so many people came that the doors had to be closed.

'Zurich has never had a move like this – there are over a thousand in the meeting – the doors had to be closed before we began. Faith has so risen in the hearts of the people that there is a great manifestation of God's power – hundreds are being saved (one hundred came forth in one meeting a week ago). The cry is tremendous, God is answering prayer. I am still broken – the power of God was so great, I could not minister but broke down and wept because of the need of the people. I did not want to do this, but the thought of the opportunity and the fact that it would be met melted me down before God.

A Bishop among many called to see me. The Lord is preparing a great harvest. The Swiss sister writes [that] hundreds cannot obtain admission to the meetings and we have had to take a larger hall.'

A later report from Miss Nelly Ruff gives some details of these meetings:

'The meetings lasted for a fortnight, and we may say that it has been a perfect success. One of the largest halls in town was taken.

A lot of advertising has been done, handbills etc., and boys parading sandwich-boards, which were quite a new thing in Zurich; the first day the people so crowded round the boys that the traffic was stopped and quite a commotion caused in the streets. Already the first meeting in the large hall with a spacious gallery was packed.

It was lovely to see from the platform all the eager faces, then they would rise and with uplifted hand utter their petitions to God – a very inspiration for anyone standing there. Mr. Wigglesworth was full of the Spirit of God declaring the full four-square gospel.

After the meeting people would crowd into a vestry to be prayed for. It was heartbreaking to see them throng around us, some halting, others bearing on their weary faces the cruel marks of sin and suffering – all eager to hear how they could approach God and claim their deliverance. Oh! The expressions of their eyes! How they changed! Scores of those sick ones went away praising God that he had healed them and saved their souls from destruction. Hallelujah.'

She went on to report that her father had continued to use the hall for gospel meetings on Sunday afternoons.

A little later, in sending a further report, she was able to tell how the work went after Wigglesworth left for his meetings in Ceylon.

'We are very busy these last few weeks; our meeting has greatly increased. Thank God the tide is rising. We have not had a meeting since Mr. Wigglesworth's visit in which there has been no healing or decision for the Lord. We have also lovely reports from people who have used handkerchiefs that have been prayed over. Prayer is being answered.'

In Ceylon, where he was a speaker at special Easter meetings, such was the success of the meetings held in a newly-built hall in Maradana that the venue proved to be too small to accommodate the crowds and larger premises had to be used, and Wigglesworth had to extend his stay. People representing all classes and all ages came from all over the island. There were many reports of healing given by the local papers, including one of a major who held a responsible position in the court. In meetings in Colombo ninety were converted.

One night a woman came up the aisle walking in great pain, her body completely doubled up. Finally she fell on the floor in front of the platform because the pain was so great. Wigglesworth jumped off the platform, put his hands on her and said, 'In the name of Jesus, I bind this pain and loose this woman.' Immediately she began to run up and down the aisle. She then sat down in one of the seats where she listened to the message free from pain.

Another outstanding feature of these meetings was the extensive use of handkerchiefs (and other garments) that were prayed over before being taken and laid on the sick who were unable to be present at the meetings. Missionary Walter. H. Clifford told this colourful story, which was used mightily for the glory of God.

'Handkerchiefs and garments were brought in an ever increasing pile, and were piled high upon the platform, so many were brought, quite five hundred some nights, so that a fairly large suitcase was necessary to hold them all; all sorts and conditions of people brought handkerchiefs and garments. Coloured handkerchiefs, silk ones, white ones, dirty ones, pieces of cloth pillow cases, and many things.

One night while our attention was diverted, a boy stole six new handkerchiefs that had been brought to be prayed for; a couple of nights later he brought them back, confessing that he had not been able to sleep since he had taken them away.'

Wigglesworth arrived back in London on 18 May, a few days after the end of the General Strike, which had lasted for nine days from 4–12 May. The main purpose of his return was to minister at the planned convention in the Kingsway Hall, London, during Whit week, which that year ran from 24 May. What meetings they were! In one of his sermons Wigglesworth said,

'Many of you know as long as 12 or 14 years ago, we used to gather with small companies of people and Divine healing was a small thing in those days, but as we lived and moved among the people they were healed and they are healed today.'

He went on to tell them:

'All over the world I tell the people that since the Lord healed me over 30 years ago, I don't know what it is to have a body. Hallelujah! It is redemption in all its fullness, no neuralgia, no stomach trouble, no kidney disease, no dyspepsia, no rheumatism, Hallelujah! No lumbago, no corns, absolutely and entirely a new order of things. This is the inheritance of all who seek Him, this is the inheritance there is in Jesus.'

The meetings were further enhanced with the ministry of Stephen Jeffreys, whom Wigglesworth was happy to introduce for the evening meetings. Another Welshman, Tom Mercy, leader of the influential Crosskeys Assembly, also contributed to the meetings by sharing some of the testimonies of healing that had taken place in his own assembly. Wigglesworth was always glad to rejoice when he heard of the results that occurred as a consequence of other men's ministry.

George Jeffreys had also been present at some of the meetings in Kingsway. On 3 July 1926, Wigglesworth wrote to him after paying a visit to the newly opened Elim Bible College in Clapham. Wigglesworth had also been to the Hampstead Bible School run by Howard Carter. He complained to Jeffreys that in Hampstead the students were crowded into small rooms 'like peas in a pod'. As the Elim college had only opened in January for its first term, there were only a small number of students. The college, a former Redemptorist Convent, stood in four acres of grounds and must have appeared luxurious by comparison. Wigglesworth boldly suggested that the two colleges should unite, with Howard Carter as the Principal. If George Jeffreys did reply, his letter has not survived, but one can imagine his consternation. He had only just bought the college and it had cost him £6,325.

Wigglesworth was no diplomat. He was a blunt Yorkshireman. But he was also a visionary. He never thought along conventional, denominational lines, not even Pentecostal denominational ones.

Chapter 14

The Depression Years

It has sometimes been argued that times of depression and industrial decline are good for religion. Learned studies have been written by impoverished students and middle-class academics on this issue, and conclusions both for and against have been reached.

After a short period (in Church history terms) of twenty years, Pentecostalism was firmly established in many parts of the world. Though widespread it had not at that time achieved the massive growth that was to lead to it becoming known as the 'Third Force' in Christendom.

In Britain, during the years 1926–30, there was a good deal of activity amongst the various groups of Pentecostals. George Jeffreys successfully pioneered large new churches in England, Scotland and Wales. His brother Stephen drew huge crowds in such places as Manchester, Sunderland, Doncaster and Bishop Auckland in the north of England. After his father's very successful mission in Bristol, Stephen's son Edward (1889–1974) pastored the Bristol church from which he established his own group of Bethel Churches. During this time Stephen Jeffreys made a brief stopover in Canada and the United States en route to New Zealand and Australia. On his way home he visited South Africa for the first time.

The traffic was not all one way. At Easter 1926 Aimee Semple McPherson visited Britain and took part in the Elim meetings being held in the Royal Albert Hall for the first time. She returned again two years later for a series of meetings in that same hall before undertaking a tour through Britain where she preached to large crowds in England, Scotland and Northern Ireland.

Smith Wigglesworth was on very good terms with Aimee McPherson and she invited him on several occasions to preach at her Angelus Temple in Los Angeles. This magnificent building, with accommodation for 5000, was pioneered by Aimee and built in 1923. Wigglesworth sometimes filled the pulpit for several weeks during Aimee's absence. In 1927 she invited him to give a series of lectures to the students in her Bible school. Fortunately, these lectures were recorded by stenographers and have recently been published.[1] They reveal another side to Wigglesworth's ministry that might otherwise have been overlooked. Here we have a man without any formal education at all giving a series of Bible studies and lectures lasting a period of several weeks. Not only this, but in an almost unique case, he allowed the students to fire questions at him, apparently without any prior notice being given. His 'off the cuff' answers reveal him as a man with his feet very firmly on the ground. He is no 'tub thumping' extremist but a man of God dispensing words of wisdom to a group of students in training for future Christian work.

Here is just one example of his teaching to the students, given on 21 July 1927:

'Don't go mad on preaching only on the baptism of the Holy Ghost. You will be lopsided.

Don't go mad on preaching water baptism. You will be lopsided!

Don't go mad on preaching healing. You will be lopsided!

There is only one thing that you will never go lopsided on, and that is the preaching of salvation. The only power is the Gospel of the kingdom. Men are not saved by baptism, not even by the baptism of the Holy Ghost, and especially not by the baptism in water. They are saved through the blood and preserved by the blood.'

The country 'fit for heroes', which had been the dream of the postwar world, never materialised. The General Strike of 1926 brought particularly severe hardship to the mining communities in South Wales. It was so bad that the official magazine of the British Assemblies of God, which had always carefully avoided making any comments of a political nature, subsequently found it necessary to appeal to its readers to send gifts to relieve the distress amongst the miners.

The economic difficulties did not restrict Smith Wigglesworth, however, and he was able to visit Australia once again. In Richmond Temple, Melbourne, he invited those who were sick to remain for special prayer when they would be anointed with oil (cf. Mark 6:13; James 5:14). In many of the meetings, however, he adopted the practice, first used in Sweden, of praying for people en masse. One report describes how he went about this:

'Brother Wigglesworth would pray for all who would stand up and believe that the Lord would heal them. He would say to the congregation that he would count to three and at the time he would say three everyone who would dare to believe and receive healing were to spring to their feet and cry out to God that they received deliverance in Jesus' name. The response to this method was always most hearty for it would be after a rousing sermon on faith and all were aroused to bestir themselves. Many testified to being healed in this way.

Another method used was to ask anyone to sit and who had pain while he prayed for them from the platform. The first meeting on the opening Sunday witnessed this method.

A lady arose saying she had pains in her head and gallstones causing suffering. When Brother Wigglesworth prayed the power of the Spirit upon her so she could not stand. When she was free to answer she said her pain was all gone. So with others in this way.'

The report included several testimonies of healing, together with the names and addresses of those who claimed to have been healed.

After leaving Australia, where he was accompanied by his daughter, Alice Salter, he went by ship to Vancouver. The weather was very rough and huge waves broke over the ship. Wigglesworth slept through most of the storm but was woken by the commotion caused by some of the ship's structure being dislodged. In spite of the inclement weather conditions during part of the voyage he continued his ministrations at every opportunity, distributing copies of his book amongst the passengers and praying for the sick. One of those healed was a Salvationist.

Returning to Britain in 1928 he ministered once more at the convention in Kingsway in May. He spoke on 'Love and the Gifts of the Spirit'. It seems as if he was allocated half an hour for ministry as he was only one of several speakers. Shortly after this he spent a further ten days in London, during which time he preached at services held in a large tent pitched in the grounds of St Saviour's Church, Crouch Hill. The vicar, Rev. W.H. Stuart-Fox, sent in a highly complimentary report. He noted in particular the number of men, both young and old, who were attracted to the meetings and testified to the fact that there were many healings.

Other conventions and special meetings were held in such places as Hull and the Lake District. At each place his ministry found a ready acceptance as he inspired faith in those who heard him. Yet for all of that it is clear that there was a limiting factor in some places. For all his widely reported undoubted success, there seems to have been a certain caution on the part of the leaders of some of the small missions who invited him to minister.

One such mission was a small Pentecostal meeting in Derby which had existed for a number of years. Its leader, Mr C. Flower, was highly regarded and held an executive position with the Assemblies of God. However, when his church asked Wigglesworth to come and conduct a series of meetings for them, they arranged for the services to be held in a small hall in a back street. There was next to no advertising aimed at attracting the general public at all. In an unusually frank and honest report, an anonymous writer confessed: 'Twelve months ago the Derby Assembly consisted of less than thirty members, with a room up a flight of stairs in a back street.' After visits from many leading ministers they had managed to build up the numbers. They had therefore planned that Wigglesworth's visit would be for the purpose of building up the spiritual lives of the believers. 'To come to this latest effort we aimed at a campaign for uplifting the spiritual tone of the members, and consequently did not advertise unduly nor take a larger hall.' The writer then goes on to admit how the response exceeded all their expectations:

'The campaign was not very old before it was realised that a larger hall would be essential for Sunday services. A larger hall was taken, and the numbers present justified the venture.

The meetings were just fifteen steps heavenward; it seemed just like one step of faith after another. No one could hear such messages and be the same again. Time after time, the whole meeting yielded to the pleading for a deeper and fuller consecration of life, and the constant exhortation to "Believe God" and to exercise the faith we have, however small ... If anything were especially emphasised it was the necessity for holiness, and the phrase: "The measure of power is in exact proportion to the measure of holiness," was reiterated time after time.

Some of the healings beggar description. It did one's heart good after one meeting to see a little boy enjoying a frolic who previously had been unable to walk unaided. One man, whose foot was damaged in an accident, a bone being displaced, felt it go back, and declared it was quite all right. Another one, a woman, who was waiting for an operation to have part of her foot removed, stated she was completely healed. And, most amazing of all, a man who was bent double, who could not stand unaided, who suffered from encephalitis lethargica (sleeping sickness), walked up and down the room praising the Lord.'

During May 1929 Wigglesworth responded to renewed calls from Norway and Sweden where he had made such an impact eight years before. He was asked to return to Norway by T.B. Barratt, the father of European Pentecostalism, when they had met up in America. When they saw each other again during Barratt's visit to Britain, the date for his visit was fixed and Wigglesworth began in Oslo on the Sunday before Easter. Easter was a very busy time for the Norwegians and so three meetings were planned for the two holy days, Shrove Tuesday and Good Friday, when offices, factories and public places were closed. Large crowds gathered. The Oslo church, with seating accommodation for 2,000, had grown rapidly under Barratt's ministry so the organisers tried to book the larger Lutheran Hall, seating 4,000. Permission would only be granted if Barratt would agree to there being no speaking in tongues, something he was not prepared to do.

Barratt, who had been born in Cornwall and received part of his education in Taunton, Somerset, acted as one of Wigglesworth's interpreters. In a report he said:

'Mr. Wigglesworth needs a couple of interpreters, as his powers of endurance are enormous. It is only the power of the Holy Spirit that can make a man hold out, meeting after meeting, as he does, and, of course, humanly speaking, a wonderful vitality and physical strength ... God has mightily used him, and his magnetic way of getting at the people explains to some extent the wonderful interest there is amongst them for his meetings. But as already stated, the chief reason is the fact that he is filled with the Holy Ghost, and has a Faith that never gives way to the wiles of the devil, but faces all opposition in a firm, but beautiful spirit, that inspires others and gives them a real lift on the upward line.

It is really inspiring to see a man somewhere about seventy years old travelling about the world with this glorious Gospel of Salvation for body, soul and spirit.'

Moving on to Bergen there was a great response and many people came to the meetings filling the largest halls that were available. Some nights converts crowded the front of the hall, many of them in tears. On one occasion several members of the music band who occupied the platform were baptised in the Spirit and spoke in tongues. The meetings continued for a week and much good was done.

Wigglesworth moved on to Haugesund, a fishing town on the west coast where once more there were such large crowds that some were unable to get into the hall. On the Sunday afternoon there were so many people that Wigglesworth and his interpreter were themselves unable to get in through the door. They had to go round another way so that they could be lifted up through a window that took them straight on to the platform. Many received healing in these meetings.

After this he moved on to Stavanger, the fourth largest town in Norway, where the Labour Party Hall was crowded every night. Again there were converts and healings reported. Calling in at Bergen for two further meetings he returned to Oslo, where he joined William Booth-Clibborn, grandson of General William Booth, at a convention.

The meetings in Sweden brought him first to Gothenburg where there were three Pentecostal assemblies, Gilead, Salem and Smyrna. At the meetings, which were held in a circus, several remarkable healings were reported. One lady, who had suffered for twenty-four years with a damaged knee as well as from what was described as an internal disease, came forward to be prayed for and was instantly healed.

He also preached in Malmo in the southern part of Sweden before proceeding to Stockholm. The Philadelphia Church in Stockholm, where Lewi Pethrus was pastor and at that time had a membership of 4,000, was the largest Pentecostal church in Europe. In anticipation of the expected crowds, they hired a larger auditorium for the evening meetings. Even then many were disappointed because they could not get in.

Before returning to England Wigglesworth preached in Westeras, Linkoeping and Joenkoeping. During this time he met some of those who had been healed on his previous visit eight years ago. One of these was a blind girl who was twelve years of age at the time of his visit in 1922. She was still perfectly whole. In one of his sermons he confirmed that he had met her. He also said that he often did not hear of healings that had taken place until after he had moved on.

Another incident that occurred on his first visit to Sweden in 1922 was related in two different sermons. Having arrived at his first preaching appointment after a long and difficult journey by ship and by train:

'As I entered the building a man fell across the doorway in a fit. I rebuked the devil in Jesus' name, and the man got up. I said, "Give your testimony." He obeyed and said it was as if something snapped from the top to the bottom of his body, and he was free. This incident was the key to open many doors of opportunity. Seven years later I was again at that place. I asked if

any remembered. A man rose in the gallery and said,
"It was me, and I have been free since."' '

His travels later in the year took him back to Switzerland
in July before proceeding, accompanied by his daughter
Alice, to Canada and the United States of America in
September.

Note

1. *Smith Wigglesworth Speaks to Students of the Bible*, compiled by Roberts
   Liardon (Tulsa, Oklahoma: Albury Publishing, 1998).

Chapter 15

In Triumph and in Trial

The past few years had been difficult economically and socially in Britain and in other parts of the world. The next three years were to prove to be years of great trial for the evangelist. For almost the first time in his life he would be forced to curtail his activities through being incapacitated by weakness caused by his own sickness.

Being healthy and staying healthy would seem at first sight to be a prerequisite for anyone who claims to have a healing ministry. Failure in this area has sometimes brought forth the cry, 'Physician, heal thyself.' One of the most successful of the American healing evangelists, Jack Coe (1918–57), who drew huge crowds in what was said to be the largest gospel tent at that time, died suddenly of polio before he was forty years of age. The man who had been leader of Dowie's work in Britain, Harry Eugene Cantel, died prematurely of peritonitis in 1910. Others, such as Charles Price (1887–1947) and F.F. Bosworth (1877–1958), lived to a good age and both remained in active ministry to the end.

Whatever the Apostle Paul's 'thorn in the flesh' may have been, it is clear that he sometimes had to face up to the fact some of those with whom he worked were sick. Trophimus was left sick at Miletus (2 Timothy 4:20) and Timothy was advised to take a little wine for the sake of his stomach (1 Timothy 5:23). Yet Paul had seen many mighty miracles of healing occur throughout his ministry (2 Corinthians 12:12; Acts 19:11, 28:8–9, etc.).

Smith Wigglesworth, in spite of his age, continued a very busy life with constant travel in all sorts of weather and crowded meetings. He continued to rise early in the morning, he still took a cold bath every morning and, whenever possible, he would have a brisk walk. He was by any account in very good physical condition for a man of his age. He kept all his own teeth. When the Swiss dentist, Dr Emil Lanz, had challenged him during his visit there, the man seems to have taken this as a testimony in favour of Wigglesworth's stand on healing. Wigglesworth had believed in divine healing since 1897/8. As we have seen, according to his own testimony he had, for the first fifteen years, experienced an unbroken record of God's love and power in healing. In November 1933 he wrote, 'For over 45 years I have believed in Divine healing, and for 30 years have been helping needy sufferers; my preaching has been to establish faith amongst the saints.'

Apart from a few references to a feeling of tiredness at the end of a long mission in some distant land, and then only in terms of looking forward to a long sea voyage and the rest that it would bring, he seems to have been in robust health, despite his age. He was always conscious that he was on his Master's business and engaged in both private and public witness.

Suddenly, in 1930, he found himself for the first time having to refuse invitations to minister. The reason for this was that he was sick. He was in considerable pain and discomfort with kidney stones. This condition persisted for three years. During the onset of this condition he continued to minister to others and he saw many receiving help and healing, yet he himself suffered agony. Eventually, after more than two years and after being sometimes prostrated with pain, he consulted a doctor. The doctor, after examining him, told him that the condition was serious and advised that he should have an X-ray. This showed that he had a stone in his bladder the size of a large bean. The doctor said that nothing but an operation would remove the stone and solve the problem. Wigglesworth told him that hundreds of people were praying for him and that he would rather die than submit to the surgeon's knife.

In spite of his difficulties at this time (his housekeeper, Mrs Steele, died on 14 March) he left on 5 May 1931 for Sweden, Norway, Denmark and Finland. He was accompanied by his friend Thomas Myerscough (1858–1932) of Preston. In each country they had wonderful meetings. In Sweden on some occasions there were as many as 400 who came forward for prayer for healing. In many of the places they visited people came forward to testify to the fact that they had been healed when Wigglesworth had visited their town, ten or two years before.

Shortly after he recovered he preached at the opening of the extension of John Nelson Parr's Bethshan Tabernacle, Manchester, over the second weekend in November. The following week he left for meetings in the United States following a further brief visit to Switzerland.

On 4 October 1933 at 4.00 p.m. his deliverance began. For the next few hours he began to excrete a quantity of grit and a number of stones. He retained nine of these as a reminder and a testimony.

It had been a difficult time for him. The man who emerged from the ordeal was a kinder, more compassionate person. He testified:

> 'I have been refusing calls for three years on account of this suffering, but now I am free and loosed from my suffering.
>
> James 1st chapter has been a great blessing to me – "Counting all joy for the trial of [your] faith worketh patience."
>
> Now I am full of praise to God for the miracle He has wrought in me. To Him be the glory.
>
> I believe the future will be greater than the past to help those who are sick and suffering.' [1]

During this period, though he was considerably restricted, his sermons continued to appear regularly, particularly in *Redemption Tidings*.

Wigglesworth's experience of being filled with the Holy Spirit had sustained him for forty years of ministry. In triumph and in trial; in tears and in pain. What could so easily have been stumbling stones became stepping stones. His ministry and the consequences would yet have an even wider scope.

Note

1. *Bible School and Missionary Review*, Vol. XIII, No. 10, 15 November 1933.

Chapter 16

Fifteen Extra Years

When Hezekiah, King of Judah in the eighth century BC, was healed of what had been a terminal illness, he asked God to give him another fifteen years of life. Smith Wigglesworth's condition may not have been life threatening but it was certainly debilitating. With his recovery he was to be given another fifteen years of ministry.

The results of his return to a more active ministry are reflected in the first report in the January issue of *Redemption Tidings* of 1934:

'Brother Smith Wigglesworth, full of life and fire after his miraculous healing, conducted two weeks' services at Mount Olivet Assembly, Preston Road, Lytham, commencing November 14th. Every meeting was a time of refreshing from the presence of the Lord. Testimonies were given of immediate relief from pain as soon as our dear brother laid his hands upon the sufferers. The Assembly desired the meetings to continue, but owing to calls elsewhere, Bro. Wigglesworth was obliged to refuse but promised a later visit.'

The same paper announced that 'Mr. Smith Wigglesworth is now rejoicing in Divine health and vigour, and is open to conduct special meetings and campaigns in any part of the country. Assemblies desiring his ministry should write to him at 70 Victor Road, Bradford, Yorks.'

In July there were further meetings in Norway and Sweden. In Bergen a woman who had been unable to walk for a number of years was brought to the meeting by car. After prayer she was able to walk.

Wigglesworth followed this with a month of meetings in Switzerland that took in five different places. After returning home to Bradford he sailed to the United States of America on 13 October. He began with meetings at Glad Tidings Tabernacle in New York. Robert Brown (1872–1948) and his wife Maria had founded this very successful church in a former Baptist church within a stone's throw of the Central Post Office, which they had purchased. Stanley Frodsham sent a report of these meetings to the British papers:

'A young girl came into the meeting for the first time because she heard of Bro. Wigglesworth through a friend of hers. She had a dislocated hip for about six years, and for two years out of the six she had to be carried around. She couldn't even use crutches. On account of her dislocated hip her one leg was about six inches from the ground. Bro. Wigglesworth prayed for the first time and he told her to walk, but she was kind of scared to walk alone; then he prayed for her again and her hip was a little better. Then he told her to remain on the platform and to believe God would heal her. He prayed again, and praise the Lord – she walked just like any one of us.'

In a later letter to Donald Gee, Robert Brown wrote:

'We have closed a very successful campaign with Smith Wigglesworth and the Salters. He not only seems a new man physically, but spiritually has ever-increasing power. We had some of the most remarkable meetings in Glad Tidings Tabernacle while he was here. At times the place was filled with God until it would be hard to describe the miraculous operations of God's power. Many got saved while he was with us, and we had some miraculous healings. In short, it was old Wigglesworth with new power.'

He was present at the opening of a new hall in Jamaica, Long Island, New York. The pastor, Vernon Gortner, wrote an enthusiastic report:

'The meetings with Bro. Wigglesworth will never be forgotten. God's power was manifested in a remarkable way, not only in healing of the sick but in salvation of lost souls. Every night there was a good altar response, and a number of folks boldly stepped out and came to the altar and accepted Christ. There were also a number of remarkable healings. One person testified afterwards of being healed of gall-stones of many years' standing. Another testified that they were healed of double rupture after suffering intense pain for years.'

On 1 March there appeared one of the most detailed descriptions of a Wigglesworth meeting. Most of the previous reports were all too brief and one had even said, 'There is no need for me to describe the meeting; we all know

Brother Wigglesworth!' James H. Taylor of West Roxbury, Massachusetts, tells of the meetings that were held in the Old Fashioned Gospel Tabernacle, 505 L. St., N.E., in Washington, D.C. He had learned about these meetings from a Mrs Taylor who had been healed some nine years ago after reading Wigglesworth's book *Ever Increasing Faith*. When Mr Taylor arrived at the church he found that the doors were closed. There was a placard bearing the words, 'Last two meetings of Smith Wigglesworth transferred to Masonic Temple.' His report continued:

'When we reached there at 2.45, a large poster on the outside announced, "City Wide Healing Services." The hall was being filled rapidly, 800 or more gathering. The song service was delightfully informal magnifying the power of the Name, the Blood of the Cross, and the friendship of Jesus.

Brief testimonies followed. One brother in a most clear and forceful voice said, "I was a sufferer from catarrh in the most virulent form. I had great difficulty in breathing and speaking. I tried all the doctors and all the healers without relief. Someone advised, 'See the Englishman.' I did last week, and God has marvelously healed me. Glory to his name."

After a reading from the Gospel of Mark, James Salter, Wigglesworth's son-in-law, told how he had been healed many times during his service in the Belgium Congo (Zaire). He went on to say, "But, if I had never been healed, and if I had never seen anyone healed, I'd believe in it, because the Bible says so."

Wigglesworth's text was, "Fear not; only believe."

His first appeal was to those who desired salvation and about twenty people responded. After this he asked those who were seeking healing to assemble in the space between the platform and the wall on the left of the hall. One hundred people responded. Turning to them he said, "Look at me and listen. I want this thought [to] take possession of you, 'I'm going to be healed!' Think of it and believe it. Second. Be sure to understand that I have never healed anyone, and I never saw anyone heal another, but I have seen the power of God work through men and heal. Hallelujah!"'

The report continues with a detailed description of what followed:

'He came down from the platform, and reaching the head of a long line, he began to lay hands upon them, commanding diseases and demons, in the name of Jesus to depart from them. They shook when he touched them, some jumped, some shouted, some were prostrated and many testified to healing.

I think it will help our testimony to state that we had seats in the second row (front) from the healing corner, so that what happened during the healing hour was almost within hand reach. Just before the meeting began, we had noticed that a young girl, with crutches, was coming in, assisted by a man and woman. Her legs absolutely dangled, with the feet hanging vertically from them. From her waist she seemed to be limp and powerless. Room was made for her in the front row. When the invitation to be saved was given, she attempted to go forward aided by her assistants. Brother Wigglesworth, on seeing her start, said, "You stay right where you are. You are going to be a different girl when you leave this place." When the rest had been dealt with Brother Wigglesworth turned to the girl and, having been told her trouble, said to the people, "This girl has no muscles in her legs; she never walked before." He laid his hands on her head and prayed and cried, "In the name of Jesus Christ, walk!" Looking at her, he said, "You are afraid, aren't you?" "Yes," she replied. "There is no need to be. You are healed!" He shouted, "Walk! Walk!" And praise God she did – like a baby just learning. Twice she walked, in that characteristic way, the length of the platform. Glory to God. When we left the room her crutches were lying on the seat, on reaching the sidewalk we saw her standing, as others do, talking with two girl friends.

The woman who assisted her forward was her mother, and the man was her uncle, who wept like a child during her healing, who testified in the evening meeting that she walked up the stairs at her home without assistance, repeated the fact that she had never walked before, stating also that her mother, who went forward for healing for a bunch in her breast, when asked about it said, "It's gone!"

Wonderful things happened in the evening meetings also. Our brother testified to healing of cancer of two years' standing. A poor sick man whom the doctors had given up, whose legs were useless, except for slow motion, was healed and ran twice around the hall. When asked how many had been healed during the week's services, at least two hundred rose.'

He ended his report by telling how he combed through the many local papers the next morning to see if any had carried a report either in a headline or even some other place. There was not a word to be found anywhere.

From New York Wigglesworth made his way to the other side of the country where crowds gathered at Bethel Temple, Los Angeles. Among the many helped was a Jewess who responded to the gospel and shortly after was baptised in the Spirit and spoke in tongues.

On his return to Britain he was the convener at the Fifteenth Preston Convention in April. It was noted that he had 'just returned from a strenuous campaign in the United States' but that he 'ministered with his usual vigour and in the power of the Holy Spirit.'

Through the rest of the year he had engagements in many different parts of Britain. In May he ministered at the Embankment Mission Anniversary services in Camberwell. At Whitsun he returned to Sunderland where he ministered and prayed for the sick. T.B. Barratt was also there at the same time. In July he spent six days in genteel Tunbridge Wells and in August he was one of the preachers at the Hull Convention. On Sunday 1 December in nearby Halifax nine people professed salvation.

There is a telling contrast between the tremendous impact of the overseas trips with their vast crowds and the noticeably smaller meetings in Britain. It is perhaps worth noting that a prophet is often without honour in his own place of origin. Yet, Wigglesworth's willingness to preach, exhort, encourage and pray for the sick in meetings large or small, and places near or far is striking. He was deaf to the clamour of the crowds, impatient with the trappings of so-called successful ministry and, therefore he was willing to take all opportunities to proclaim the full gospel of a saving, healing and delivering Lord. His criteria for ministry were not the size of the crowds, the prestige of the pulpit or the extent of the offering but simply obedience and faithfulness to the leading and directing of the Holy Spirit.

Chapter 17

Fruitfulness in Old Age

Around this time there were a few people living on the fringes of Pentecostalism who subscribed to the idea that true believers were somehow endowed with immortality and they would not die. They had produced a number of pamphlets in which they sought to argue their case. Donald Gee, joint editor of *Redemption Tidings*, found it necessary to write an article to refute these arguments. In the course of the article he pointed out that some well-known preachers had lived to a great age. John Wesley was still preaching several times a day when he was well past eighty; George Muller was still preaching after he was ninety; Laurence Chaderton, one of the translators of the King James Version of 1611, remained in active ministry past the age of 100.

In 1936 Smith Wigglesworth was seventy-seven years of age. He never tried to make any secret of his age, in fact he regularly referred to how fit and well he was. As he grew older, those who reported on his meetings increasingly drew attention to his advancing years. The invitations continued to find their way to his home in Bradford. In addition to his regular round of visits to the larger conventions, he received many invitations from small Pentecostal assemblies in Britain.

Although he had travelled extensively in Europe, the United States of America and Australasia, up until this time his only visit to any part of Africa had been a short visit to Palestine and a stopover in Egypt. Of course, he had already had strong links with the continent, both through the work of his daughter and son-in-law in the Congo and the great contribution he was able to make through the funds he channelled into missionary work.

Other Pentecostal evangelists had been to Africa and had found a fruitful field for their ministry. John G. Lake (1870–1935), who had first gone there in 1908, spent four years in the country. Stephen Jeffreys (1876–1943) went there for the first time in 1929. His first meetings, which in Durban were held in a tent, attracted large crowds of blacks, whites and others from diverse ethnic backgrounds. Jeffreys moved on to Johannesburg, and at meetings in the City Hall, despite the fact that he found it difficult having to be translated into three different languages, there were many healings. He was invited back again in 1932 and spent most of the year there. Not long after his return to Britain his health suddenly deteriorated and in March 1935 he curtailed his meetings in Becontree and eventually returned home to Wales where he spent the remaining years of his life in quiet seclusion. Regrettably some writers have suggested that Jeffreys became proud as a result of his success in South Africa. One writer reported him as having said, 'The world is at my feet', and drew the conclusion that, as a result of his pride, God struck him down with sickness. The foundation of this story, which has since been repeated in another publication, was a remark that was made by Jeffreys when he saw the huge crowds arriving at his meetings (although crowds of similar sizes had been present in Sunderland and other places in England). It was not pride that motivated this remark: it was more a momentary panic, 'What shall I do with all these people?' It has to be said that of all the modern evangelists, both of that time and since, there was none more humble than Stephen Jeffreys (except possibly Smith Wigglesworth). Why a Christian brother should pass on such a story I do not know, except perhaps a paranoid fear of clerical attire and Christian organisations. It surely tells us more about the one who perpetuated the story than it does about the one of whom the story was told. But, worse, what does it say about the Almighty, or rather people's concept of Him? Even if the evangelist was proud, which I would dispute, would a loving God treat His servant in such a manner after using him with such powerful effect for more than twenty years?

It is probable that, with the sudden and unexpected removal of Stephen Jeffreys from the field, others were invited to South Africa. Amongst these was Fred Squire (1904–62), who was emerging as a promising young pioneer evangelist with the British Assemblies of God. Squire left, with his wife, on 6 November 1936 to begin ministry in South Africa.

Smith Wigglesworth was in Cape Town from 26 October until 3 November, beginning his meetings at Durban Avenue, Salt River, and then moving to the Town Hall. The local press gave good coverage of the meetings, including a number of photographs. The *Cape Times*, dated 2 November 1936, carried a favourable report:

'More than 2,000 people, who crowded into the City Hall yesterday afternoon, were witnesses of the most amazing evangelistic meeting that Cape Town has known.

A 77 year-old world evangelist, Mr. Smith Wigglesworth, who arrived in South Africa recently under the auspices of the Apostolic Faith Mission, conducted the meetings in the City Hall.

The meeting lasted for two hours, and long before the starting time almost every seat in the main hall and in the gallery was occupied. It was a cosmopolitan audience in which all classes – rich and poor – were united in the common bond of Christianity.

The preacher, a grey-haired man with a moustache, was an impressive figure on the platform, and he called upon those who wished to be healed and who believed that they could be healed through faith and the power of God, to stand up.

Almost half the congregation was on their feet in a few seconds. He prayed for them, and told them to place their hand on the portion of their bodies afflicted. Hundreds declared that they had been cured by the first prayer. They sat down, but those who felt that their ailments had not been cured were told to come to the front.

With tears in their eyes, gesticulating with their hands and sobbing aloud, more than 300 men, women and children crowded to the front of the hall.

The preacher took off his coat, and in his shirt sleeves walked off the platform, taking up a position on a chair as the crowd strode past him out of a side door into the passage to return to their seats, through the back of the hall.

When they had all filed past the preacher, he returned to the platform and put on his jacket again.

He then asked those who had been cured to testify. More than 500 people at once jumped to their feet.'

Wigglesworth then moved on to Wynberg, Cape Province, arriving there on 4 November. The minister, R. Coates, reported that in forty-six years of experience he had never witnessed such scenes of revival, nor seen such remarkable healings. He noted that Wigglesworth was tired out when he arrived and rested that day before commencing meetings in the 650-seater Town Hall, the largest available building. Even this was crowded out, with around 1000 people present. His report continued:

'There was no standing room, and the people crowded on the platform. All shades and conditions were represented. Mohammedans, Malays, Jews, Coloured, maimed, impotent, crippled, paralysed and cancerous pressed in for promised help. Mrs. Salter and Mr. Wigglesworth preached Jesus Christ as the living Word and under the unction of the Holy Ghost.

On 5th, 6th and two meetings on 8th, I should estimate that 600 stood to receive salvation through the blood of Jesus. After these conversions in each meeting, pains immediately disappeared in answer to prayer from the platform. On 6th and 8th the crowd of the 5th had increased, until those outside were as many as those inside the hall. Never had Wynberg had such a visitation, and never had the need of the healing touch of Jesus been so manifest, and God met us and the need.

I have in my study the crutches of one coloured girl, crippled, but healed instantly. One elderly man, whom I assisted into the hall, so bound with rheumatism that he could not sit, flourished his crutches in the air as God immediately met him in prayer and he walked triumphantly out of the hall. In four cases of terrible cancer the pain ceased immediately hands were laid on the sufferers. The halt walked normally, deaf ears were unstopped and the blind saw. One paralysed Jewish boy danced with joy as he left the hall.

Our difficulty will be to find a large enough hall to contain the hungry crowds when our brother and sister return early in March.'

The 29 January issue of *Redemption Tidings* carried a further report of Smith Wigglesworth's visit. This was the first report penned by David du Plessis (1905–87), the newly appointed General Secretary of the Apostolic Faith Mission. It was probably the 31-year-old du Plessis who informed the press about Wigglesworth's impending visit. Unlike some of his British contemporaries he was never shy about seeking the maximum publicity for the infant movement. In later years this would become his most significant contribution to the cause of worldwide Pentecostalism and would take him into areas that neither he nor anyone else ever expected. In fact he would go into places and would meet people with whom he would have thought that he shared nothing in common. I will return to this connection in my next chapter. His report tells us:

'During the past years news filtered through of how God was blessing His servant, Smith-Wigglesworth in other countries, many of God's people in South Africa prayed that he might come out here to bring the message of life. God answers prayer and there was indeed rejoicing when we were able to announce at the Easter Conference, 1936, that it might be possible for brother Wigglesworth to visit South Africa and that he might be with us at the December Conference.'

After telling of Wigglesworth's arrival in October he continued:

'The newspapers in this country are generally indifferent towards Pentecost, but they seemed to take notice of our elderly brother and gave great publicity to his meetings. It was quite a surprise to see the papers come out with pages of pictures taken in the meetings. Columns were written about the meetings, and the Cape was stirred. Mighty healings took place and in a few cases it might be said that the healings were miraculous. What is of more importance, however, is the fact that so many were swept into the Kingdom of God.'

People had come from many parts of the country to attend the December meetings. The City Hall in Cape Town was packed with 2,000 people and on the last Sunday of the Conference nearly 2,000 gathered for three great meetings in Johannesburg city hall.

Wigglesworth stayed on in South Africa until 5 March, covering vast distances while he was there. A young man who had been converted through reading Wigglesworth's book bought a Ford motor car and drove him and his party from place to place. In conservative Durban Wigglesworth preached in the four-year-old Full Gospel Tabernacle for Archibald H. Cooper, Vice Moderator of the Full Gospel Church of South Africa. Some 400 people came for the opening meeting, increasing to 600 on the final night.

In January he ministered in Witbank, Transvaal, for six days. People came from all over, some covering many miles to be at the meetings. In every place that he visited there were miracles of healing as well as numbers of converts. In some towns, like Wynberg, the local ministers continued to hold the meetings after the evangelist's departure. According to Wigglesworth's own report, 'Brother Coats and others decided to carry on, and 340 decided for Christ on the first Sunday after we left.'

At Salt River, Cape, his meetings were followed by a visit from Fred Squire in December 1936. There were twenty converts at his first meeting. A photograph, taken in David du Plessis' home and published in March the following year, showed Fred Squire and his wife, Smith Wigglesworth, James and Alice Salter and David du Plessis and his wife.

According to some later accounts, it was during this period that Smith Wigglesworth came into David's office and confronted him. Pinning him to the wall, he delivered a prophecy about the future of the Pentecostal Movement and of David's part in that Movement. It is to this that I will devote the next chapter.

Chapter 18

That 'Prophecy'

All Pentecostals believe in prophecy. There are, however, many different approaches to the subject amongst them. Some groups, almost from the beginning, have made this a major feature of their work. A number of these (though not all) are to be found amongst those classified as 'Apostolic'.

When the Pentecostal Movement was in its very early stages in Los Angeles in April 1906, the first report of what was taking place in the Azusa Street Mission appeared in the *Los Angeles Times* of Wednesday 17 April. The evening before, a reporter, on his way home after work, hearing of what was taking place in the former livery stable, called in to see what was happening. As a result his somewhat sensational report appeared on the front of the second section of the paper. Of particular interest to us is the fact that he reported someone having a vision in which the ground opened and multitudes were swallowed up. Those present interpreted this to mean that God was going to bring judgement on the city of Los Angeles. On Wednesday 18 April most of the city of San Francisco was destroyed by a massive earthquake, in which 300,000 of the 400,000 inhabitants were made homeless and 10,000 people lost their lives. The vision seemed to have been all too accurate;

the problem was with its interpretation. The interpreter was most unlikely to have seen the name 'Los Angeles' written over the name of the town; she probably just made that assumption. San Francisco was some 400 miles away.

A year later, in India a 'prophecy' was given and published which foretold that Colombo, Ceylon (Sri Lanka), would be destroyed in an earthquake. It did not happen.

Prophecy does have a place but it should be used wisely and sparingly: it must be judged (1 Thessalonians 5:19–20). A prophecy attributed to Smith Wigglesworth has in recent times gained significant interest and is now in the public domain on the Internet. This presents a number of serious problems which I would like to outline.

1. Although, years after the event, David du Plessis told the story of how Wigglesworth had come into his office and spoken the prophecy to him, he did not tell the story, or even hint at it, until Wigglesworth was dead and buried.

2. In the year that Wigglesworth died (1947) David du Plessis was one of the speakers at the Annual Conference of the Assemblies of God of Great Britain and Ireland. In his sermon to the ministers and other delegates he said many things that were completely contradictory to what he later claimed Wigglesworth told him in 1936/7.

3. There is no evidence I know of to suggest that Wigglesworth ever engaged in the business of uttering these sort of predictive prophecies. We know he was bold when it came to healing, and we have already told of occasions when he declared in public, before a large congregation, that a person who was obviously sick was going to be healed there and then.

4. The claims for the prophecy in question, after being first hinted at, were subsequently enlarged. There became more than one prophecy: the one given in South Africa during Wigglesworth's visit there in 1936–7 and another given, so it is suggested, at the very end of Wigglesworth's life.

5. The wording of the prophecy also gives rise to problems in that in its final form it includes words that Wigglesworth would not have used: thus it is anachronistic.

6. Wigglesworth's views on prophecy, such as we have them, do not encourage us to believe that he ever thought that the gift should be used in this way.

The Prophecy

The first time that David du Plessis ever wrote anything about his meeting with Smith Wigglesworth was in an introductory article that he wrote as Conference Secretary for a brochure prepared for the Third World Pentecostal Conference held in London in 1952.

'How well I remember the increased desire for fellowship when the late Smith Wigglesworth visited South Africa in 1936. One morning early he came into my office and without a word of greeting said, "Young man, you have been in Jerusalem long enough. The Lord says you have to go to the uttermost parts of the earth." I was dumbfounded. "He has much work for you and you will be going soon." Then he prayed, "Lord, let him always enjoy your blessing and never get sick on his many travels ahead."

Later he spoke to me and warned me that absolute obedience, at all cost, would be the price for having a share in the greatest revival that ever had been known in history.'

A few weeks later, in 1937, David was invited on account of his official position to attend a meeting in Memphis, Tennessee, of the General Council of the American Assemblies of God held from 2 to 9 September. Also present were Howard Carter and Donald Gee of the British Assemblies of God together with Archibald Cooper of South Africa. Many years later, du Plessis said that he had shared with Donald Gee on that occasion what Wigglesworth had prophesied to him. There is considerable confusion about much of this. In an interview he said, in answer to a question, that he had first told Donald Gee about Wigglesworth's prophecy during the second World Pentecostal Conference in Paris in May 1949. All that can be said with any degree of certainty was that Wigglesworth did say something to David when they met in South Africa. The most certain part of this was that David had 'been in Jerusalem long enough'. Such phraseology, which was a reference to Jesus' words to the disciples to 'Tarry in Jerusalem until . . . ' was well known among Pentecostals (see Luke 24:49). Such a declaration was just the sort of thing that Wigglesworth would have said in those circumstances. I am not so sure that he would have regarded his words as being prophetic, though the invitation to visit the United States coming later in the same year might seem to confirm this.

Subsequently the original reference to David was changed and the prophecy was given a different form. Some writers have also suggested that Wigglesworth gave another word shortly before he died. Here is the wording as it is now circulating in its most recent form:

'During the next few decades there will be two distinct moves of the Holy Spirit across the Church in Great Britain. The first move will affect every church that is open to receive it and will be characterised by a restoration of the baptism and the gifts of the Holy Spirit.

The second move of the Holy Spirit will result in people leaving historic churches and planting new churches. In the duration of each of these moves, the people who are involved will say, "This is the great revival." But the Lord says, "No, neither is the great revival but both are steps towards it." '

It continues with a prophecy about the coming together of the Word and the Spirit:

'When the new church phase is on the wane, there will be evidence in the churches of something that has not been seen before: a coming together of those with an emphasis on the Word and those with an emphasis on the Spirit.

When the Word and the Spirit come together, there will be the biggest movement of the Holy Spirit that the nation and, indeed, the world has ever seen. It will mark the beginning of a revival that will eclipse anything that has been witnessed within these shores, even the great Wesley and Welsh revivals of former years. The outpouring of God's Spirit will flow over the United Kingdom to the mainland of Europe and from there will begin a missionary move to the ends of the earth.'

In the various forms that have been reported, the main message would seem to be that (i) there was a revival coming that would surpass numerically all past revivals and (ii) David du Plessis would have a part in that revival.

A number of writers who have studied the subject in detail have also pointed out some of the difficulties in reconciling the various accounts. Whatever was said to David du Plessis by Smith Wigglesworth over sixty years ago, there can be no doubt that there has been a revival within the Christian Church in many parts of the world. Whether Wigglesworth said the exact words that David later recounted (which I do seriously question, for it is well nigh impossible for anyone to recall precise words spoken to them even after a few weeks, let alone after forty years), there need be no doubt that Wigglesworth believed (as most Pentecostals had done from the beginning) that there would be a great revival before the return of Christ. One of the earliest Pentecostal books was entitled *The Latter Rain Covenant* (1910). In it the author, D. Wesley Myland, writing about the use of the phrase 'latter rain', spoke of his expectation of an outpouring of the Holy Spirit in the last days, based on Acts 2, Joel 2 and James 5.

There are a number of authenticated instances where future revivals have been anticipated. John Wesley's father, Samuel, clearly spoke of his belief that God's work would revive, but that he would not see it. It was the godly dean David Howell, who in December 1902 published an article in which he said that 'The Holy Spirit religion is the only cure of the moral and spiritual diseases of Wales at this time ... the principal need of my country and dear nation at present is still spiritual revival through a special outpouring of the Holy Spirit.' In November 1904 what became known as the Welsh Revival (though there had been revival in

Wales before that time) began. In the period between November 1904 and the Spring of 1905 some 100,000 converts were recorded in Wales. Evan Roberts told his brother, Dan, before the revival started that God had promised him 100,000 souls.

The Pentecostal Revival was to be different in many respects. It was conceived on the first day of the twentieth century in a mansion. Its birth was in April 1906. Facing opposition from many established Churches its progress, with few exceptions, was not spectacular at first. Some of those who helped to spread its message had to fight a lonely battle as they sought faithfully to follow the mandate that challenged them to proclaim the full gospel, which included signs and wonders. Smith Wigglesworth, though lacking any formal education, was an inspiration not only to those of his own time but to future generations. In the time since his death in 1947, the worldwide Pentecostal Movement has grown numerically beyond even Smith Wigglesworth's wildest dreams. Perhaps, like Moses of old, he saw what lay ahead. Others who would come after him would go on to enter into that which was promised.

Chapter 19

Still Active

Wigglesworth made the most of the opportunities afforded him by his healing in 1933. On one occasion in 1937 he remarked, 'My mother said I was born kicking, and I've never been still since.' His plain, down-to-earth language is reflected in another memorable saying recorded in June 1937: 'If you only have faith you'll never be looking down your nose at your feet.' By any account it was little short of astonishing that a man of his advanced years should still engage in such an active ministry. His worldwide ministry was, however, limited by his increased age and it finally came to an end with the outbreak of the Second World War in 1939.

On his return from South Africa in March 1937 he resumed his ministry in Britain. Travelling from his home base in Bradford he responded to calls from both large and small gatherings. Whether it was to a small, struggling assembly meeting in an upper room, or as the convener of the large convention that was held every Easter in Preston he did not spare himself in ministry. He rarely preached long sermons but he continued to minister to the sick, even at times when there were very many people to be prayed for. Wherever he went, on trains, buses or ships, all over the world he witnessed to rich and poor alike. He was not just a platform man.

His worldwide ministry may have been restricted but his sermons continued to appear regularly in magazines both in Britain and in the USA. The fruits of his ministry were to be seen in many places. In January 1939 Lester Sumrall, who had recently visited Switzerland with Howard Carter, was able to report that he was aware of some nine churches that had been established in that country as a result of Wigglesworth's visit there in 1920. Though Wigglesworth's ministry in Britain was not linked with the planting of new churches he sometimes held series of meetings that continued for up to a week or more.

In the period leading up to the outbreak of the war we find him ministering in Hull and near Sheffield. In October 1941 he was reported as being 'still active, and has ministered recently in the Full Gospel Church at Leamington Spa, where twelve were filled with the Holy Spirit.'

In the following year it was recorded that he travelled alone on a crowded train from Bradford to Boston in Lincolnshire where he ministered for a few days. We can only hope that someone gave the old gentleman a seat as those trains could be very crowded. In 1943 the war dragged on with rationing, shortages and the blackout, and all of the disruption caused by evacuation. Yet, he continued to minister wherever possible. In August he was at the Ivy Church in Bristol (their minister, W. Knight, was killed on Good Friday, together with three members of the church – he was the only Pentecostal minister to lose his life as a result of the air raids in Britain). Two people were converted during his visit and many were healed, including a sister who had not walked for eight years.

In December it was reported:

'Smith Wigglesworth in his 84th year is resting at home in Bradford after completing a busy season of engagements in various places. His voice suffered, but is now improving, and he already looks forward to a great time next Easter at Preston Convention, if God permits.'

There was an obvious slowing down of his activity with his advancing age but he still took an active part in the Preston Conventions. In the Convention of 1944 he said, 'I gave my heart to the Lord Jesus when I was eight years old, and now I am eighty-five.' During the meetings, at which Donald Gee and James Salter ministered, two of the others providing ministry were the Irishman, Joseph Smith, Dean of the Elim Bible College (who was to be the preacher at Wigglesworth's funeral two years later), and George Stormont, who would write a book about Wigglesworth.

The 1945 Convention at Preston was held between March and April with meetings from Good Friday to Easter Monday. Wigglesworth was the convener as usual. The report of the meetings tells us:

'At almost all the meetings the large Congregational Church was crowded, particularly on Friday and Monday when there were about 1,000 people present ... Brother Wigglesworth had a marvellous testimony of renewed life and caught his spirit of earlier days. He told how that last year it was feared that he was passing away but God quickened to him the Scripture in Romans 8:11, and He who raised up Jesus from the dead quickened the mortal body of his servant. It was apparent to all that our esteemed brother, who is 86 years old, had a supernatural experience. Not withstanding the fact that there were three meetings each day during the four days, Brother Wigglesworth never missed a meeting, lifting the great congregation into heights of expectation by his words of faith. This living exhibition of God's quickening power stimulated the faith of all, especially those who were seeking God for divine healing.'

The convention was a great success with previous records being broken all round. Twenty missionaries or candidates for mission were introduced, and the missionary offering totalled £654, which was a considerable increase on the previous year. Some 150 were baptised in the Spirit and about twenty were converted. It was however, to be Wigglesworth's last convention.

In December 1946, Elim pastor George Steele married Francis Virr, one of the three sisters whose father was a deacon at the Elim Church in Bradford. One of the guests was Andrew Lambie, an Elim minister who, like Mr Steele, hailed from Greenock in Scotland. While he was in Bradford he went to visit Smith Wigglesworth in his home in Victor Road. The old warrior had not been well and did not get up from his bed until the afternoon. However, he invited the young man in and had a prayer with him. He told him that he had received an invitation to go back to Australia to hold meetings and that he very much wanted to go but did not feel well enough. After he died, his son-in-law told of many invitations to minister in faraway places. Robert Brown (1872–1948), co-founder of Glad Tidings Tabernacle, New York, had wanted him to preach at their Fortieth Anniversary services in May 1947. They even added the suggestion that he could travel by plane as this would be very comfortable. It was not to be.

The impression has been given by at least one writer that very few people ever visited Wigglesworth in his home. This is not true. From the earliest times the house was always open. It was not always easy for anyone to visit as he was away so frequently and one never knew when he might be at home. After he lost control of Bowland Street the house in Victor Road became a regular meeting place. In later years, however, he spent more time in Bradford where, after his housekeeper died, his daughter Alice regularly opened the door to visitors. He was never too busy to see them. Whoever came never went away without a prayer, a Bible reading and a word of exhortation.

After I had started to gather together the material for writing about Smith Wigglesworth I got into conversation with an elderly gentleman who often sits in front of me when I am in the Sunday morning service in Cardiff City Temple (where my son Christopher is minister). When I told him that I was planning to write about Wigglesworth he said, 'My mother went to stay with Wigglesworth once. She was sick. He asked her where the trouble was and he hit her. I do not know what she was suffering from, but, whatever it was, she was healed.' He went on to say that he had a letter that Smith Wigglesworth had written to his mother. It was written from Bradford on 9 January 1943.

'Beloved Sister Pugh
Your letter ... just arrived. The Lords Prayer is before me this morning[.] Not My will but thine be done[.] you and the others have and I have prayed with desire for her to be raised up from the awfull sickness but acording to His divine will and Purpose it was not to

be but will all rejoice in the Fact she kept the Faith so she will receive the Crown of life for all that keep the Faith. There is a crown of life no one can die without his will[.] See Rev 1st chapter 18 vs He has power over Death and Hell. So now you must rest in his perfect will[.] I am sorry you are suffering with Rhumatics you need good support and warm clothing[.] we will remember you in prayer[.] God bless you for all your loving kindness to the dear one you were so kind to[.] God bless you we all send love[.] yours in Him His Servant

Smith Wigglesworth'

It was a mixture of pastoral concern and practical advice to keep warm in cold weather.

The last winter of Wigglesworth's life was to see the longest and coldest spell in Britain for 200 years.

Chapter 20

A Long and Eminently Useful Life

During the very severe weather that gripped the country through the winter of 1947, covering everywhere with a thick blanket of snow and ice, Wigglesworth was confined indoors. He still continued to keep in touch with many people and a constant flow of letters came through the letterbox at 70 Victor Road, Bradford. There were many requests for ministry, as well as small packets containing handkerchiefs and the request that these should be prayed over and returned so that they could be placed upon the sick.

In the last week of his life he was still seeking to minister help and encouragement to others. George and Grace Thomas, who lived in a small village near Canterbury, had a small son, David, aged two-and-a-half. He was described as a hopeless case by the doctors who said that the boy was too weak to live. In desperation they wrote to Wigglesworth enclosing a handkerchief and asking for his prayer. He returned the handkerchief together with a letter quoting Scripture and encouraging them to believe that God would do the work. On the day the letter arrived, at the time of his afternoon rest, the mother prayerfully laid the handkerchief on his head as she put the little boy to bed. When he woke up for his tea she reported that for the first time he was able to eat properly without choking. From that time on he was able to eat solid food and his bowels functioned normally. Previously his bowels had been in a chronic condition and without medication he was in agony. Each day showed a continual improvement. When the parents heard that Wigglesworth had died they sent in this testimony which was published a month later.

On the day before he died Wigglesworth wrote to one of the Virr sisters (their father was a deacon at Bradford Elim).

'Dear Sister Virr

Many thanks for your letter received[.] All Saints are being tried[.]

This is a proof that we are His but are more than conquerors through Him. The trial of your Faith is more prescious than gold tryed in the fire[.]

On Jan 4th this year God gave me a real victory over a bad case of cancer[.] Early in the morning God gave me Luke 10:19 I will give you power over all the power of the enemy and nothing shall by any way hurt you[.] A very helples case & lost almost all flesh[,] all strength[.] could not walk or use her arms[.] The Lord's Presence was so real[.] He Himself wrought a great miracle[.] As soon as hands were put upon her she was able to walk & use her arms and no more pain. About 10 people came into the room and with one voice we had never seen any thing like this before[.] You can understand what joy & presence of God filling the house[.] So you can imagine what the house was like full of joy in the Holy Ghost...'

Thus the letter, only one page of which has survived, ends.

While the severe weather continued there were additional problems that resulted in shortages in essential supplies. Factories were closed through lack of fuel and workers were sent home. Public transport, on which many people depended, was severely disrupted owing to the large amount of snow and ice. The north of England was particularly badly affected. Restrictions were imposed by the authorities on the use of newsprint. The printing of weekly publications was banned for two weeks and as a consequence the two main Pentecostal papers were not published during part of February and March. Before this interruption, the 14 February issue of *Redemption Tidings* republished a letter that Smith Wigglesworth had sent to Alexander Boddy forty years before. The ban was lifted on 3 March. On that date the Executive Council of the Assemblies of God were meeting in Wakefield and, at the conclusion of their business, they went to visit Wilfred Richardson, a member of the Council and minister of Glad Tidings for the past twenty-five years, who had been seriously ill since Christmas. Richardson, a long-time friend of Wigglesworth, died at his home aged seventy-two years old on Sunday morning, 8 March. It was announced that his funeral was to take place at Wakefield on Wednesday 12 March at 2.45 p.m. It was to be conducted by James Salter (Richardson had been a member of the Missionary Council for eleven years).

Smith Wigglesworth, on hearing of the death of his old friend, very much wanted to go to the service at Wakefield. The family and the doctor, who had already advised him to stay indoors in the inclement weather, advised him not to go. However, another old friend, Alfred Green, minister of the Assemblies of God church at Ripon, arranged to take him. Wigglesworth, who had himself lost a young son, had

comforted his friend when he lost his youngest son
(a Squadron leader with a DFC) at the end of the war.
Knowing that the weather was cold, they wrapped him up
warmly in the car for the drive to Wakefield. On the
journey, Wigglesworth pointed out a chapel where he and
Polly had ministered on several occasions many years
before. He also recalled how he and Wilf Richardson had
journeyed together round the area ministering the Word.

When they arrived at the hall, most of the congregation
were already seated. Wigglesworth made his way slowly up
the steps to the main body of the church. One writer says
that he first sat in the second row of pews behind the
immediate family before ascending the steps leading to
the vestry on the right-hand side of the church. The
organist was quietly playing 'O, Rest in the Lord', while
the congregation awaited the arrival of the coffin. For a
moment there had been a subdued murmur as unexpectedly Smith Wigglesworth was seen to arrive and make his
way through to the vestry.

Amongst those who were waiting in the vestry for the
arrival of the cortège was the Church Secretary Mr Hibbert,
members of the Executive Council, Frederick Watson,
Donald Gee and James Salter who was to conduct the
service. Wigglesworth, who in spite of his age and the fact
that he had made the journey in such cold weather, looked
well. Seeing Mr Hibbert he enquired about the health of his
sick daughter. The Hibberts had been for a meal with
Wigglesworth just one week before. He was told, according
to such report that we have, that there was not much
improvement (which was honest). In some of the later
biographies of Wigglesworth, there is, sadly, an unfortunate
misinterpretation of this incident. One writer has suggested
that this apparent 'failure' was the last straw that killed the

old warrior. Another has proposed that it was a response to another question to a lady, whose mother had been prayed for and who was not healed, that greatly troubled Wigglesworth – that writer going so far as to add (from whence he obtained this information I do not know) that the lady said, 'Your prayers made her worse.' According to this writer, this unbelief so upset Wigglesworth that it killed him. None of those who were present at the time reported any such incident. The question we must ask is this: why should it be thought necessary for us to place the 'blame' for Wigglesworth's death at anyone's door? How can the unnamed lady be blamed, even if what she said, as unkind as it was, was untrue? We surely cannot blame the Church Secretary for telling the truth about his daughter's health. Neither can we blame Mr Green for taking Wigglesworth to the funeral. He did what he did as a favour to his old friend.

'*The Lord gave, the Lord hath taken away, blessed be the name of the Lord*' (Job 1:21). The words of Balaam were, '*Let me die the death of the righteous, and my last end be like his*' (Numbers 23:10). Wigglesworth had lived a long life. He never courted publicity for himself; he always sought to bring glory to his Lord. His life had been dramatic on many occasions; his death was also to be dramatic.

Warming himself by the open fire in the vestry, the old man exchanged a few words with those assembled there waiting to take part in the service that was due to begin in ten minutes' time, who were perhaps thinking that they must give a space for Wigglesworth to say a few words about his late departed friend. It was not to be, however. For, so suddenly, in Donald Gee's words,

'Almost his last words were a loving inquiry about the health of a daughter of the Church Secretary for whom he recently had prayed. He sat down, and then almost immediately seemed to have a kind of stroke. Three of us surrounded him, and cried earnestly to the Lord. But it was God's will to take him home. There was no pain: no struggling; it was all over in a few minutes. We could hardly persuade ourselves that he had really gone.'

Just at that moment the news came that the funeral party had arrived. The coffin was carried in by the Church Secretary's four sons. James Salter, with great dignity and presence of mind, in what for him must have been a very traumatic experience, stepped out of the vestry onto the platform and opened the service for Wilfred Richardson. After the opening hymn 'Great God of Wonders' was sung, there were readings from Psalm 23 and part of 2 Corinthians 5. James Salter then went down into the body of the chapel while the congregation was in prayer. He indicated to his wife, who was profoundly deaf, that she should follow him into the vestry where the body of her father was resting. He then returned to address the congregation. 'We have a double sorrow,' he said, 'one here,' pointing to the coffin, 'and one there', pointing to the vestry door. There was a subdued gasp from the congregation as he told them of the sudden passing of Smith Wigglesworth. Then, with some difficulty, but with a few carefully chosen words of comfort and exhortation, James Salter drew the service to a close as the final hymn 'On that Bright and Golden Morning' was sung. Fred Watson concluded with a prayer for James and Alice Salter and their family on their sudden loss.

Six young men carried the coffin of their beloved pastor from his church to the burial ground. James Salter remained behind to deal with the necessary formalities of his father-in-law's sudden death. The Church Secretary went immediately for the doctor to confirm death. If such an incident had occurred today, the coroner would have had to be informed and if the deceased person had not been seen by a doctor in the previous two weeks there would normally have to be an autopsy to ascertain the cause of death. In Wigglesworth's case, though he died away from his home town, no such formalities were called for. He had declared, many years before, that no surgeon's knife would ever touch his body. This proved to be the case, not only in life but also in death. Perhaps also on the natural level there was the undeniable fact that owing to the terrible weather conditions and the prolonged spell of extremely cold weather the number of deaths at that time was at a record level. Many of these, particularly among the elderly, were sudden (though many were considerably younger than Smith Wigglesworth).

Less than a week later, with the snow still thick on the ground, another large congregation assembled for the funeral of Smith Wigglesworth. This took place at the Elim Church in Leeds Road, Bradford, which Wigglesworth had attended for many of his later years and at which his son Seth was the Secretary.

It was not a good time to arrange a funeral. There was a backlog already owing to the number of deaths. The roads in many places were unswept. However, the falling snow kept off long enough for the service to be conducted. Fortunately help was at hand. Florence, Seth Wigglesworth's wife, had a sister whose husband was the Assistant Chief Constable of Bradford. He was able to arrange for the roads to be cleared for the funeral cortège and those who accompanied them to the cemetery.

It was an impressive service, convened by Donald Gee with solemn dignity and feeling, and with Joseph Smith (1890–1980) one of the preachers. Gee himself was a world traveller who had visited many of the places where Wigglesworth had ministered: Australia, New Zealand and the USA as well as all over Europe. They had often shared ministry together and Wigglesworth had on one occasion confessed that he owed Donald Gee a great deal. Gee was a great writer and very good teacher, but he was a very different man from Wigglesworth. Even he, with all his eloquence, found it difficult to sum up the life of his old friend. It was appropriate therefore that in his brief address he should choose as the reading Hebrews 11. 'It contained,' he said, 'his favourite subject, Faith, and even if he did not start with it, he very soon got there.'

At the end of the service four of the men who a few days before had carried Wilf Richardson to his last resting place, now carried Smith Wigglesworth. He was conveyed through the silent streets to the cemetery at Nabb Wood where he joined his beloved wife and son George. The simple inscription reads:

IN LOVING MEMORY
of
MARY JANE
The beloved wife of
SMITH WIGGLESWORTH
of Manningham
who died Jan 1st 1913
in her 53rd year
'I am the resurrection and the life'
also of their son GEORGE
who died March 22nd 1915 in his 19th year

and of the above
SMITH WIGGLESWORTH
who died March 12th 1947 in his 88th year
I have fought a good fight. I have kept the faith II Tim 4:7
Whose faith follow Heb. 13, 7

A number of years later, the words were added: 'And of Alice, daughter of Smith Wigglesworth and wife of James Salter who died Dec 21st 1964 aged 80 years'.

Thus we come to the end of the long and eminently useful life of a man who continued his ministry to the last. In our final chapter we will give a few tributes to his ministry from some of those who met him in his later years.

'Four generations'. Back row: Seth (left) and Leslie.
Front row: Brian (Leslie's son) with his great grandfather, Smith Wigglesworth

From:-
70, VICTOR ROAD,
HEATON,
BRADFORD, Yorks.

March 11 — 47

My Dear Sister Virr

Many thanks for your Letter Received
All Saints are Being Tried this a Proof
that we are His but we are more than
Conquerors thrue Him the Tryal of your Faith
is more Precious then Gould Tryed in the Fire
on Jan 4th this year God Gave me a Reel Victory
over a Bad Case of Sicea Early in the morning
God Gave me Look 10.19. I will Give you Power
over all the Power of the Enemy and nothing Shall
by any way Hurt you a very Helpless Case at Last
almost all Flesh all Strength Could not walk
or use His arms the Lords Presence was So
real He Himself wrough a Great Miriacle
as soon as Hands was Put upon Her She
was able To walk & Use His Arms and no more
Pain about 10 People Came into the Room
and with one Voice we have never Seen
any thing like this Before you Can understan
what Joy & Presence of God filled the
House So you Can Jus Emegin what
the House was like full of Joy my this Reply

The last letter Wigglesworth wrote to one of the Virr sisters (their father was a deacon at Bradford Elim). Wigglesworth died the next day.

Wigglesworth family gravestone at Nabb Wood, Shipley, Yorkshire.

Desmond Cartwright (right) and Roberts Liardon (left) at Nabb Wood in 1988.

Chapter 21

Tributes to an Apostle of Faith

Hardly anyone who met Wigglesworth ever forgot that meeting. It is a great pity indeed that not more people recorded their recollections of this humble apostle of faith. Here I have added tributes from two ministers who have fond memories of him.

The first is Tom Walker, who met Smith Wigglesworth as an eighteen-year-old recently arrived in Bradford from his home in Hull. He had moved there in order to serve as assistant to the minister of the Elim Church, William Hilliard. Later Tom Walker would serve with distinction in the Elim Pentecostal Church, eventually holding the highest office of General Superintendent.

'In September 1942 I was appointed as assistant minister at the Bradford Elim Church, then meeting in their 950 plus seater building known as Southend Hall, Southend Street. The congregation numbered 160 or so in the morning and 250 on Sunday evenings, despite war-time restrictions, including the dreadful nightly black-out. A faithful, beloved Sunday morning supporter was Mrs. Alice Salter, Smith Wigglesworth's daughter ... Smith Wigglesworth, though advanced in years, pursued an indefatigable itinerant teaching and faith-building ministry throughout the United Kingdom. They were rarely home at weekends...

I can recall Smith Wigglesworth's ministry on only one Sunday morning during my eight month's stay in Bradford. His simple, forceful, Bible-based style was greatly in evidence.

His son, Seth, a gifted musician, and director of the family plumbing business, was the Church Treasurer, while his grand-daughter Millie (Amelia), was a regular, much-appreciated soloist. Every meeting at the church was incomplete if someone at least did not pray for "our Leslie" and "our Cissie."

My special memories, however, refer to two notable occasions when the senior pastor of the Bradford Church, William J. Hilliard and his wife, Ann, and I were invited to tea with Alice Salter and her father. Alice served the meal of bread and butter (probably including margarine then as the ration was 2 ounces of butter and 4 ounces of margarine per person per week!) and some of that must have been her home-made jam and cakes.

The conversation was relaxed, occupied with the things of God. When we had eaten, the great man, who was dressed in one of his three suits, black in colour and including a waistcoat with deep pockets (a real preacher's suit!), took a small Bible out of one of the pockets. Fixing his pince-nez fairly well down his nose, the renowned Apostle of Faith said, "Well, now we'll have a word with Father!" He read from the Scripture and proceeded to expound it for about ten minutes. He then declared, "Well, now we'll talk to Father." His prayer ranged widely over God's work at home and overseas.

My special unforgettable benediction came when he prayed, "Now, Father, bless this young man!" He proceeded to intercede for me with great warmth and care. It was like being blessed by a patriarch of God. It was the same on both occasions.'

Leon C. Quest was minister of the Elim Church in Bradford in the last years of Smith Wigglesworth's life.

'It was in 1937 that I first met Smith Wigglesworth. I got onto a train at Huddersfield station. I was making my way to my home in Plumpton, Devon, where my father was very ill. Wigglesworth was sat in the compartment with his daughter, Alice. A young man entered the compartment smoking a cigarette. "Get out!" said Wigglesworth. "No smoking allowed here!"

I introduced myself to him as pastor of the Huddersfield church. He had heard of me through his son Seth, who was about to do some work for us on our new building in Huddersfield. We shared a time of fellowship and I told him about my father who had once been a believer. "I'll pray for him," Brother Wigglesworth said. The remarkable truth was that my father came back to the Lord on the following day. I was with him when he died.

The next time that I met him was in 1946 when I became minister of the Bradford church. He sometimes worshipped with us. I would ask him to give a word at the Sunday morning meeting. We had introduced individual deaf aid equipment. Alice Salter, who was deaf, appreciated this. One Sunday morning, when Wigglesworth was ministering on the theme,

"Have faith in God", I told him to keep near to the microphone. He kept walking away. Alice would beckon to me to tell him to move back. I would touch him and he would return to the microphone.

Very often at 9 a.m. on a Monday there would be a knock at the door of our house. I would hear his voice calling, "Where's that boy?" Off we would go on the bus to Baildon Moor, near the place where he was born and where he worked as a young boy. One morning that I remember we got on the bus, he paid the fare. Often on these journeys he would shout, "Glory!" This day he began to speak in tongues. The conductor asked me, "What is he saying?" I replied, "He's a foreigner!" On another occasion we were roaming around the moors on a very narrow road. Wigglesworth said, "Let's sit here and pray. You pray first." Closing my eyes, I did so. Then, as I heard him beginning to pray, I heard the sound of a car coming. Opening my eyes, I looked right into his face. His eyes were wide open. Later I asked him about this. He said that in the Congo they always keep their eyes open when they pray, they have to watch out for the restless people. He said, "The Bible says, 'Watch and Pray.'"

In the early part of 1947, the Elim Missionary Society held an exhibition in Bradford. I took George Thomas, the Missionary Secretary, to see Smith Wigglesworth who had not been well and was in bed. Looking at me, he said to Mr. Thomas, "I love that boy, but I hate that thing around his neck" (meaning my clerical collar).'

No single testimony could fully do justice to the unique man or to the extraordinary ministry that was Smith

Wigglesworth. Certainly all he lived for was to receive from his Master a 'well done, good and faithful servant.'

We may not be able to help ourselves wanting to know the secrets of Smith Wigglesworth's life, meetings and ministry. Yet, we must do so seeking not just simple formulas but an encounter with the same Holy Spirit who filled the life of a rough and ready plumber and empowered him to take the message of faith in Jesus Christ to a lost and needy world.

If you have enjoyed this book and would like to help us to send a copy of it and many other titles to needy pastors in the **Third World,** please write for further information or send your gift to:

Sovereign World Trust
PO Box 777, Tonbridge
Kent TN11 0ZS
United Kingdom

or to the **'Sovereign World'** distributor in your country.

Visit our website at **www.sovereign-world.org**
for a full range of Sovereign World books.